IT'S A BIG DEAL!

Real Deal bible studies

faith issues

CONCORDIA PUBLISHING HOUSE • SAINT LOUIS

AUTHORS

Beth Balzer

Chris Drager

Gretchen Foth

Tim Frusti

Jeanette Groth

Rich Gutekunst

Barrie Henke

Joan Lilley

Mary Meyer

Jay Reed

Nikki Rochester

Tom Rogers

Mark Sengele

EDITOR

Mark Sengele

Scripture quotations are taken from the HOLY BIBLE, NEW INTERNATIONAL VERSION®. NIV®. Copyright © 1973, 1978, 1984 by International Bible Society. Used by permission of Zondervan Publishing House. All rights reserved.

Quotations from Luther's Small Catechism are taken from Luther's Small Catechism with Explanation, copyright © 1986, 1991 Concordia Publishing House.

Photos on pages 14, 68, 76, 84 used by permission of LCMS District and Congregational Services Youth Ministry Office. Photos on pages 32, 38: comstock.com

This publication may be available in braille, in large print, or on cassette tape for the visually impaired. Please allow 8 to 12 weeks for delivery. Write to the Library for the Blind, 1333 S. Kirkwood Road, St. Louis, MO 63122-7295; call 1-800-433-3954, ext. 1322; or e-mail to blind.library@lcms.org.

Your comments and suggestions concerning the material are appreciated. Please write the Editor of Youth Materials, Concordia Publishing House, 3558 S. Jefferson Avenue, St. Louis, MO 63118-3968.

Manufactured in the United States of America.

1 2 3 4 5 6 7 8 9 10   13 12 11 10 09 08 07 06 05 04

table of contents

INTRODUCTION

WELCOME TO THE REAL DEAL SERIES!

Welcome to the Real Deal! Each of the books in this series presents 12 lessons that focus on the Gospel and the Word of God, the Real Deal. Each book in the series has a theme around which the lessons are organized. (For an outline of the Real Deal Series, look inside the back cover of this book.)

* *The topics* are real. Each lesson deals with real issues in the lives of young people and is grounded in God's Word.

* *The leader's materials* are easy to use. Each lesson is completely outlined and designed for real success in teaching. Leader's directions are clear and easy to follow. Materials needed for teaching are easily obtained. Many lessons contain additional materials for times when students finish quickly.

* *Student pages* are reproducible so teachers can copy the number they really need.

* And, finally, the **power of the Gospel** is at the core of every study. Students will see God's Word as the real source of information for their everyday lives.

ABOUT THIS BOOK

It's a Big Deal!

Each of the 12 studies in this book deals with issues concerning their own faith or the faith of others that many young people face. Many of these issues can be very sensitive for young people to deal with. Use care in your approach to each study so that God's truths remain objective and your care for each student becomes personalized.

The studies are designed for use with students in the ninth through twelfth grades. More mature junior high students may also benefit from these studies. Each study is a complete unit. Lessons may be used in any order. While designed for the typical one-hour Bible class, these studies may be adapted for other youth ministry settings. For example, selected studies could form the core of material for a youth night or retreat.

PREPARING TO TEACH

Each lesson has a *Lesson Focus* and a *Gospel Focus* statement at the beginning. These help the leader understand the lesson topic and direction.

The *Lesson Outline* provides a quick look at the study and a list of materials needed for each segment of the lesson.

The *Lesson Activities* include large- and small-group discussion, opportunities for individual study, and active-learning suggestions.

Most lessons also contain background information to assist the leader in preparing for the class time. Class leaders should review the entire lesson in advance of the class time.

It is assumed that the Bible class leader will have the usual basic classroom equipment and supplies available—pencils or pens for each student, blank paper (and occasionally tape or marking pens), and a chalkboard or its equivalent (whiteboard, overhead transparency projector, or newsprint pad and easel) with corresponding markers or chalk. Encourage the students to bring their own Bibles. Then they can mark useful passages and make notes to guide their personal Bible study and reference. Do provide additional Bibles, however, for visitors or students who do not bring one. The appropriate Student Page should be copied in a quantity sufficient for the class and distributed at the time indicated in the leader's notes.

The studies are outlined completely in the leader's notes, including a suggested length of time recommended for each section of the study. The suggested times will total 50–60 minutes, the maximum amount most Sunday morning Bible classes have available. Each session begins with an opening activity that may or may not be indicated on the Student Page. Teachers who regularly begin with prayer should include it before the opening activity. Most other parts of the study, except the closing prayer, are indicated on both the Leader Page and Student Page.

An average class size of 10 students is assumed. To facilitate discussion, especially when your class is larger than average, it is recommended to conduct much of the discussion in smaller groups—pairs, triads, or groups of no more than five or six. Instructions to that effect are often included in the guide. If your class is small, you are already a small group and can ignore any such suggestions.

Some lessons contain bonus suggestions. Use these when the study progresses more quickly than expected, when your normal session exceeds 50–60 minutes, or when a suggested activity doesn't work with your group. Students can also use them during the week.

Of course, the leader is encouraged to review the study thoroughly, well in advance of its presentation. Then the materials can be tailored to your individual students' needs and preferences as well as your own preferred teaching style.

TIPS FOR LEADERS OF YOUTH BIBLE STUDIES

One challenge of leading a youth Bible study is the need for relevant, Christ-centered material. An equal challenge is growing in one's ability to teach and lead effectively. While the studies in the Real Deal Series are intended to meet the first challenge, the following tips are intended to help you meet the second challenge. Skim this section for ideas that spark your interest, or read it completely. Either way, you'll find support to help young people grow in God's Word.

BIBLE STUDY THAT CHANGES LIVES

It is not an oversimplification to say that a major goal of Bible study is to change lives. Since this is so, our success in teaching may lie partly in knowing what in Bible study will produce change.

Scripture testifies that all people are sinful and, as a result of their sin, are spiritually dead (Romans 3:23; Romans 6:23). As these statements of God's Law confront us, we come to the certain knowledge that we cannot rescue ourselves from spiritual death. We need a Rescuer. Through the Gospel, the good news of salvation through the bitter sacrifice and death of Christ, God rescues us from eternal death and gives life. Through that same proclamation of the Gospel we receive power to overcome sin and temptation. Through the Gospel the Holy Spirit empowers and equips us to serve God in word and deed. As Paul writes in Ephesians 2:8–10, "For it is by grace you have been saved, through faith—and this not from yourselves, it is the gift of God— not by works, so that no one can boast. For we are God's workmanship, created in Christ Jesus to do good works, which God prepared in advance for us to do." Our good works are good because they come from Christ at work in us through faith.

What does this mean for our teaching? It means that as we teach (empowered by Christ at work in us), the best life applications will be those motivated by the Gospel—the proclamation of forgiveness and strength through faith in Christ. Using the Law for motivation sets the students up for failure. "We should pray more/study the Bible more/be kinder to our neighbor" doesn't work because we can't—not on our own, not without help. "Follow the example of Peter/Joshua/David/even Jesus Christ" doesn't help—we are not Peter, Joshua, David, or Jesus. "Follow these three biblical principles" doesn't work—we can't follow the 10 God gave us.

What will work? Students need to hear the Gospel. Every class session is an opportunity to remind them that God loves them, that He sent His Son, Jesus Christ, to die for them and wipe them clean of all their sin—that through the faith worked in us, Christ is already at work. Hearing the clear Gospel message and having sure knowledge of their forgivenness will make a difference in their lives. Only the Gospel can change lives.

Will students grow tired of hearing it? Only if it is repeated in tiring ways. Our challenge in each lesson is to find the Gospel power and apply it to our students' lives in fresh and meaningful ways. Good material will help; being constant in our own Bible study and spiritual growth will help. And we can rely on the power of Christ at work in us as teachers to make it happen. God's blessings as you teach!

STRUCTURING YOUTH BIBLE CLASSES FOR GROWTH

Can structure and organization contribute to or hinder the growth of a Bible study program? The American church-growth movement over the past two decades or more has contended that they can. Applying principles of sociology to Bible classes cannot substitute for interesting and biblical teaching, but when coupled together, these create a climate for expanding your Bible study ministry. The following suggestions are not the "last word"; follow them only where they make sense for your congregation.

Multiple, Age-Group Defined Classes

Think in terms of several classes. You may not need six or twelve separate classes right now, but structure your program so that multiple classes are possible when needed. Depending on your facilities, ideal class size is probably six or more students. Young people may be self-conscious in very small classes; only the most highly motivated will return regularly to a class of three. Establish a new class for each grade level, combining years as necessary to average six or more students each week. Be prepared to split combined classes as attendance grows. In a large church this may mean six to twelve classes; in a smaller church, perhaps only two or three to start.

Think Long-Term

Encourage the classes to adopt a long-term identity. Identify them as "Mr. Schultz's class" or the "Saints Alive" class or the "Class of '06" rather than the Junior High class or the tenth-grade class. A long-term identity that will not change each year or after a couple of years will build a mind-set for regular attendance and commitment.

Build Ownership

Where possible, encourage the class to choose and recruit their own Bible study leader. When the young people have a voice, they will also have more commitment to the class. When an adult leader knows that the youth themselves chose him or her as someone they wanted to have as a leader, they are more willing and motivated. Allow the "permanent" leader to invite short-term "guest speakers" to add variety, but encourage him or her to attend even when a guest leads class.

Make sure that Bible study leaders know (1) what they are to do (their specific duties); (2) what they are to teach (how materials are chosen and purchased); (3) how they can grow in their skill (provide training opportunities and materials); and (4) when they will be invited to "reenlist" (be specific; no life sentences allowed). If possible, provide this information in writing as a job description.

Allow young people to welcome visitors and introduce new class members, to develop a follow-up program for visitors and absentees, to plan their own quarterly social activity outside of class time, and to select their own mission project. These activities will build ownership, provide youth with responsibilities and leadership training, and improve the authenticity of the welcome and follow-up. They will need the assistance of the leaders or staff. Young people are capable of and probably willing to do these activities with help and encouragement.

Allow students to participate in selecting their study material. Provide them with several good alternatives that are acceptable to your church and the Bible study leader. Involve the leader in the process of choosing. Set a goal for each class to choose a study or training program related to outreach or evangelism at least once each year.

"Births" and "Deaths"

Plan to start at least two new classes every year: an entry-level class (for students being promoted from lower grades into the youth Bible study program) and one class that combines two grade levels.

Allow classes to die gracefully when required. A class that no longer draws six or more students on a regular basis and has had no new members added during three months may need to be assimilated by another more vigorous group. Classes will have life spans just as all living things do. Be prepared to start a new class to replace the one that ends.

Recruiting Bible Study Leaders

New classes will require new leaders. Existing classes will occasionally also require new teachers. In a society where people guard their time even more than their money, a good recruiting technique is a must. Here are some tips:

* *Identify candidates carefully. Not everyone can teach. And you don't want just anyone. Invite the class members to suggest candidates they know and respect from the adults of the congregation. Ask your pastor for the names of mature Christians, whether new to the congregation or longtime members, who might relate well to youth.*

* *Select the best possible candidate from your slate. Pray for guidance. Look for strengths. Look for reasons that person might be motivated to serve.*

* *Don't ask for a "blank check." Give your candidate a written description of the task, an honest estimate of the number of hours a week it will require, and a specific term of service. Be realistic and accurate. Do not overwhelm the new recruit.*

* *Guarantee success! Provide orientation and training. If you are a retiring leader, consider introducing, training, and supporting your replacement for a few weeks as you finish your service. Have a support system for weekly contact and assistance. Monitor the first few weeks of teaching carefully to spot problems early.*

* *Provide support and appreciation. Find a way each month to express, or have someone else express, honest appreciation for the new leader's work.*

* *Debrief with the Bible study leader about eight weeks before his or her term of service is complete. Offer another term of service, or ask for help to rewrite the description of the position or communicate with the new leader.*

* *Serve with joy! Your joyful service will be a bright light to those that follow.*

i'm mad at god:
is that okay?

LESSON FOCUS

Being mad at God is not unnatural for people, even Christians. In fact, Christians may experience being mad at God more often than non-Christians. Through this study participants will identify things that can make them mad at God, rejoice that God's grace and forgiveness are greater than their sins, and develop a stronger confidence in God despite what may be happening in their lives.

GOSPEL FOCUS

Through Christ, our great Redeemer, God forgives all our sins and develops such a strong bond of hope and confidence within us that we can say with Job, "Though He slay me, yet will I hope in Him" (Job 13:15).

Lesson Outline

ACTIVITY	SUGGESTED TIME	MATERIALS NEEDED
Opening	5 minutes	Newspaper or magazine articles
Job's Life	15 minutes	Copies of Student Page, Bibles
Job's Lament	10 minutes	Copies of Student Page
Job's Consolation	10 minutes	Bibles
Myth or Truth?	10 minutes	Copies of Student Page

OPENING (5 MINUTES)

Greet each student. Post some accounts (from newspapers or magazines or make up your own) that depict Christians suffering. Discuss how such situations make us feel. For example, ask, "How could Christian parents of a young child killed by a drunk driver feel about God?" (Students will likely respond that a natural reaction may be one of anger at God.)

JOB'S LIFE (15 MINUTES)

Share the following information with the class as time allows.

Job 1:1 describes Job as a man who was "blameless and upright; he feared God and shunned evil." Job was a devout, God-fearing individual. God also blessed him with great wealth. "He had seven sons and three daughters, and he owned seven thousand sheep, three thousand camels, five hundred yoke of oxen, five hundred donkeys, and had a large number of servants. He was the greatest man among all the people of the East" (Job 1:2–3).

Satan came onto the scene, and strange things happened. God pointed to Job and remarked what an upright and God-fearing person he was. Satan responded by saying that he ought to be because he had it made. Satan told God that if the wealth were gone, Job would curse God to His face. God allowed Satan to take away his wealth and family. Yet, Job remained firm in his trust of God. Satan then received permission to strike Job with fierce sores from head to foot. Job was in utter misery, yet he did not lose his faith. However—Job was mad at God.

Ask, "Have you ever been mad at God? If so, what caused you to be mad? When you had a chance to think about being mad at God, how did you feel about it?" Direct students to share their stories in groups of three to five each.

Distribute copies of the Student Page. Direct students to Job 19 and the Student Page questions. Skim the chapter with your class, pointing out Job's reasons for anger (nearly every verse has at least one).

Redirect the students to verses 7, 10, and 22. Encourage them to find three serious complaints Job makes. Again use small groups so that every student has an opportunity to share his or her responses. Then invite each small group to report on one of the complaints. Likely responses are listed here:

Verse 7—Job got no justice when he cried out; in fact it was as if God did not even listen to his cries.

Verse 10—Job got hit from every direction, so much so that he was losing hope of any better treatment.

Verse 22—Job had the feeling that God was relentless in His attack and there was no relief in sight.

JOB'S LAMENT (10 MINUTES)

Direct the students to discuss the questions in their small groups. Share the following comments with the class.

Job was a devout worshiper of God. He knew that he was a sinner and that sin had consequences. But He also knew God to be gracious and compassionate, forgiving sin and rescuing His people. Job was frustrated to the point of rage because he felt God was "out of character" in allowing his suffering.

Job's friends encouraged him to search deeply within himself for sin that deserved great punishment, but Job knew in his heart that God wouldn't typically act that way. According to Job's thinking, God was not showing His great mercy, and if Job could only argue his case in front of God, he would win.

JOB'S CONSOLATION (10 MINUTES)

Continue with Job's story on the Student Page. Read or have a volunteer read Job 19:23–27. Job did not understand why God allowed terrible things to happen to him. But God is God, and His will and ways are beyond our understanding. God by His grace had built such a strong bond or relationship with Job that even all his distress could not break it. In his utter agony, Job cried out with the words of faith that inspired our great Easter hymn, "I know that my Redeemer lives" (verse 25). Job realized with complete confidence that the eternal salvation of God's people is assured. They may experience trouble, pain, even death—yet the hope of salvation and the resurrection of a new body are assured. With his eyes of faith Job could see the Last Day, the great day of the resurrection of all flesh, and he was confident that he, too, would rise and join his Redeemer in life everlasting.

At the end of the book God did take away Job's suffering and blessed him again, giving him twice as much as he had before. And he once more had seven sons and three daughters. The daughters were more beautiful than all other women in the land. Job lived another 140 years and saw his children and their children to the fourth generation.

MYTH OR TRUTH? (10 MINUTES)

Remind the students of their own experiences of anger with God. They may not know the end of the story, but through the Spirit they may experience an abiding faith in God and in the salvation that Christ Jesus won for us.

Divide into small groups. Then direct the small groups to discuss the four items listed under the heading "Myth or Truth." Allow groups to report their conclusions. As you discuss their responses, incorporate the following comments.

1. *Truth—Sins do have consequences. This is also true for Christians whose sins are forgiven. For example, in a sinful rage, you may strike out and injure another person; you can be truly forgiven for that sin, but the consequence of the injury remains.*

2. *Myth—We are all sinful, but by God's grace Christians are declared "not guilty." The Bible clearly teaches that the wages of sin is death. Death is precisely what we would be liable for if our sins were not forgiven. But when God in Christ forgives our sins, He also removes the guilt. We are freed from the eternal penalty of sin. That is why the Gospel of Jesus Christ is such good news. It declares that we are not guilty.*

3. *Myth—Pain, distress, and loss are not always direct consequences for specific sins that Christians commit. These are part of life in a sin-fallen world. In fact, there may be no connection whatever between a pain or loss and a particular sin. God sometimes permits painful things to happen in our lives according to His will and for His own good purpose. The bottom line is that God does not allow us as His people to suffer for no reason. Even though His reason may be hidden from us, we can have confidence in the God who works for our good in all things (Romans 8:28).*

4. *Half-truth/Half-myth—Being mad at God is not unnatural, but it is sinful. When Job was confronted by God for his words and rage, he humbly repented (Job 42:6). It is important to emphasize that being mad at God does not in and of itself break the saving relationship with God. Job would have been saved even if he had died during one of his outbursts; Job never lost faith throughout his time of severe testing. It is finally faith in Christ Jesus, our Redeemer who lives, that saves us. But it is this same faith that drives us to try to root all sin, including being mad at God, out of our lives.*

Close with prayer. Acknowledge that we sometimes think we know better than God what should or should not happen in our lives. Also invite the students to share prayer thoughts that have developed during this study.

1. i'm mad at god: is that okay?

Job's Life

Job was a man who was mad at God. Skim through **Job 19:1–22** and identify some of the more than two dozen reasons why Job was mad at God. According to the following verses, what made Job's condition even worse?

Verse 7:

Verse 10:

Verse 22:

Job's Lament

According to **Job 19:1–7** Job maintained that his fate in God's hands was not consistent with God's love. What do you think? Did Job have reason to be mad at God? Why or why not?

Job's three friends Eliphaz, Bildad, and Zophar encouraged Job to identify and confess his great sin. They assumed that his distress was a result of sin. What do you think?

Job's Consolation

Job found no relief or hope in arguing about "fairness" or "lack of fairness." Read **Job 19:23–27.** What was Job's consolation?

Myth or Truth?

1. For a Christian all sins still have consequences.

2. For a Christian all sins still carry guilt.

3. For a Christian all pain, distress, and losses are consequences of specific sins.

4. Being mad at God is unnatural and sinful.

anger with god

god nurtures our relationship

LESSON FOCUS

Worship is this kind of communication between God's people and the Author and Object of their love. As we gather around Word and Sacrament, we are nurtured in our relationship with God and grow in faith in His Son, Jesus Christ.

GOSPEL FOCUS

We cannot force young people to want to go to church and Bible class. But God, through His means of grace, can change hearts. He will forgive our sins of bad attitudes toward worship and reluctance to attend. He promises many blessings through His Word. Through worship we are reunited with all the saints, spiritually refreshed, and empowered for our place in His kingdom. As young people experience God at work through the preaching and studying of His Word to strengthen faith and give power for daily living, they will be enabled to make God-pleasing choices.

Lesson Outline

ACTIVITY	SUGGESTED TIME	MATERIALS NEEDED
Worship Is . . .	*10 minutes*	*Newsprint or whiteboard and markers*
Why Church?	*15 minutes*	*Copies of Student Page, Bibles*
God's Part/Our Part	*20 minutes*	*Copies of Student Page, hymnals, service bulletins*
Making It Personal	*10 minutes*	*Copies of Student Page, Lutheran Worship*

WORSHIP IS . . . (10 MINUTES)

Divide a whiteboard into two parts or tape two large sheets of newsprint to the wall. On the left write the words "Worship is . . ." As students arrive, have them complete the sentence on the right portion of the board or sheet. When all have arrived, have them react to each other's comments. Allow them to express both positive and negative thoughts.

WHY CHURCH? (15 MINUTES)

Direct students' attention to the "Why Church" section of the Student Page. Give them a few minutes to complete their responses. Then ask them to share their answers in groups of three to five students. When the groups have finished, invite reports from each.

Some of the whys from Hebrews 10:19–25 include confidence in our relationship with God (verse 19), to draw near to God in faith (verse 22), to be forgiven and cleansed (verse 22), to be encouraged in our hope and the promises of God (verse 23), and to encourage each other toward love and good actions (verse 24). As your students respond, point out that God wants us to come to church to grow in our relationship with Him. The Sacraments of Baptism and Holy Communion are visible signs of His love for us. Through them He provides forgiveness of sins and eternal life. We receive from them the various benefits listed in the Hebrews passage. For a refresher you might want to read "The Sacraments" in Luther's Small Catechism and these verses: Matthew 26:26–28; Titus 3:5–8.

GOD'S PART/OUR PART (20 MINUTES)

Direct your students' attention to Exodus 29:42–46. Have someone read it aloud while the rest follow along. Explain that the Tent of Meeting was the early worship site for the Israelites. It was there that sacrifices would be made and God would "meet" and "speak" with His people. In response, His people would bring sacrificial offerings. Through the vehicle of worship God directed the Israelites in their relationship with Him. Worship continued to develop as a relationship between God and His people throughout the Old and New Testaments and is expressed in many forms today. Worship consists of two parts: God revealing His great love for us in Jesus Christ and our response to that love.

Distribute representative hymnals or service bulletins from your church and direct the students' attention to the order of service. Working in groups of four, have them identify under the "God's Part" heading all the parts of the service where God communicates His love for us. (These may include the announcement of forgiveness after confession, the Scripture readings, the sacraments of Baptism and Holy Communion, the message of the sermon, the benediction, and other parts of the liturgy.) Under the "Our Part" heading, have them identify all the things we do in response to His love. (These may include confession, prayers, responses, songs, and offerings.) Give them 5 or 10 minutes to work through the orders of service in the bulletins and hymnals to make their lists. Then get their input and compile a master list on newsprint or the whiteboard.

Explain that just as God met His people in worship at the Tent of Meeting, so He meets with us in worship today. In worship God communicates His love for us as we hear the Good News of Jesus' life, death, and resurrection through teaching, preaching, and the Sacraments. And we respond with songs of praise, prayers of thanks, and our tithes and gifts for His service.

MAKING IT PERSONAL (10 MINUTES)

Ask, "What happens in a relationship if one person does not do his or her part?" (The relationship is less than it could be. It may diminish or even die away.) Challenge your students with the thought that their worship relationship will grow through their active participation. Say, "God is communicating His love for us in every worship service we attend. Is our relationship with Him growing? We can look at this two ways. First, are we ready to receive what God wants to reveal to us in the service? Second, what kind of response will we offer?" Judging from their responses to the "Why Church?" sheet, you will be able to sense your students' attitude toward worship in your church. It is often difficult for teens to get excited about traditional worship services because they do not understand why the service and music are the way they are. In an age of rock, rap, and MTV, worship can seem irrelevant and boring. Help students see the majesty and awe of worship by sharing the words concerning worship in the introduction to *Lutheran Worship* found at the front of the hymnal (pp. 6–7).

Challenge your students to reflect on the part of worship they have the most control over—their attitude. Direct their attention to the "Making It Personal" section on the Student Page.

Have students work alone to complete the two sentences by listing two things they can do to enhance their worship. The first response should be something they could do to actively hear God's love for them, such as "make a note of words of forgiveness" or "look for God's promise to us in the Scriptures or sermon." The second response should be something they could do to demonstrate their gratitude to God, such as "try to sing songs I'm not familiar with" or "bring some money to put in the offering plate." Emphasize that these things can happen not because of their own efforts but because of the enabling power of the Holy Spirit working in them.

Close with prayer. Invite students to offer prayers that thank God for His love and ask His help to respond by following through on the things they wrote on the Student Page.

2. god nurtures our relationship

why church?

Take a look at **Hebrews 10:19–25.**

List all the blessings you can find that God has for us:

god's part   our part

making it personal

I can better understand God's love for me in worship by . . .

I can respond to His love for me by . . .

worship

3

OUR CATHOLIC HERITAGE

LESSON FOCUS

Young people are curious about the differences among various denominations, particularly those they encounter among their friends and acquaintances. Using God's Word as a standard, young people can confess their own faith clearly and compare it with the beliefs of others without belittling them.

GOSPEL FOCUS

Students can give thanks for the strengthening of their faith that takes place through the study of God's Word.

Lesson Outline

ACTIVITY	SUGGESTED TIME	MATERIALS NEEDED
Warm-Up	5 minutes	chalkboard or newsprint
Let's Compare!	20 minutes	Copies of Student Page, newsprint, markers, tape
What Scripture Says	15 minutes	Copies of Student Page, Bibles
Faith Conversations	10 minutes	None
Closing	5 minutes	None

A NOTE TO THE LEADER

This study was written with some important truths in mind that you will want to remember as you teach.

1. Roman Catholics and Lutherans believe that Jesus Christ came to earth in human flesh, to die in payment for our sins so that, by His grace, we are saved. Both churches are Christian churches.

2. Both the modern Roman Catholic Church and the Lutheran church evolved from the same church of the Middle Ages and before that the early church, or the first Christians. Many of the abuses of the Middle Ages have been addressed in the Catholic church just as they have in ours.

As you teach don't assume that modern Roman Catholicism is the same as that of the Middle Ages or that all you've heard about the practices of Catholics represents the official teachings of that church. Don't argue that "they don't believe the Bible" or belittle their teachings because they interpret Scripture differently than we do. Avoid stereotypes, speak gently about weaknesses, and present their teachings fairly. Guard against being highly critical, especially of teachings you may not fully understand.

Check out the instructions under "Let's Compare!" before the day you plan to teach the lesson. This activity can be more interesting with a little advance work on your part.

WARM-UP (5 MINUTES)

Ask students, "What words, ideas, or images come to mind when you think of the Roman Catholic Church?" Write all answers to this question on newsprint or a chalkboard.

When suggestions slow down, ask, "Where have you learned these ideas about Catholics?" (Students may suggest a variety of sources. These may include conversations, visits with friends and relatives—things they've overheard or seen depicted in movies and television, etc.) "Are they all accurate or true?" (Students will likely admit that they don't really know enough to verify that all they know is true.) Then say, "Let's look at specific teachings of the Roman Catholic and Lutheran churches."

LET'S COMPARE! (20 MINUTES)

Distribute the Student Page. Prepare a sheet of newsprint for each of the topics on the Student Page. Write the topic heading at the top of the sheet. Starting halfway down the sheet, write the summary printed below. Fold the bottom up to cover what you have written, and fasten it with two small pieces of masking tape, leaving the top half exposed and blank. Post these pages on the walls of your classroom. Give each group a marker and have them write their description on the top half of the page.

More information is available from many sources. Check with your pastor, DCE, or local library for books on these subjects.

Direct the students into groups of two or three. Let each group select one of the teachings in this section of the Student Page and ask them to prepare a description of what your church teaches about that item. After a few minutes, ask each group to share what they have written. After each report, share the information below.

The Reformation: Martin Luther didn't initially want to form his own church, just to reform the error that existed in it. The Catholics eventually reformed many of these nonscriptural teachings and practices after the Protestants broke away. But many practices based on church tradition are still taught.

Salvation: Catholics believe in salvation by grace through faith in Jesus Christ, the same as Lutherans do. Yet many Catholic believers still think that their personal actions play a part in their salvation.

Lord's Supper: Catholics teach that the bread and wine become the body and blood of Jesus. Bread and wine are no longer present, only the body and blood. Lutherans teach that the body and blood are present "in, with, and under" the bread and wine.

Baptism: For Catholics it is a means of grace through which God brings faith, the same as it is for Lutherans.

The Bible and the Apocrypha: Catholics and Lutherans believe that the Bible is the norm for all belief. No doctrine may contradict the Bible. The Catholics include a few additional books, called the Apocrypha, in the Bible. Lutherans believe those are helpful books, but Lutherans don't believe they are inspired by God.

Purgatory: When a person dies, according to Catholic teachings, he or she spends time in a place called purgatory, where that person is purged of earthly sin. Some Catholics believe this is not a place, but an event that happens instantly. Some Catholics believe that praying for the dead will get them out of purgatory faster. Lutherans believe that Christians are already fully purged of sins because of the sacrifice of Jesus.

Private confession: Catholics believe private confession is necessary. The problem is that Catholic believers may feel coerced into confession and penance, believing that through their penance they "work out" part of their salvation. Martin Luther wanted to continue private confession, and it is, in fact, available to Lutheran Christians. Yet Luther also urged public confession as a regular part of worship.

Mary and the saints: Catholics esteem men and women of great faith as people we should imitate. They are not worshiped, but many Catholics pray to them, believing that these saints can intervene and pray for us now in heaven. Lutherans recall the lives of saints, believers who have gone before us, looking to God's action in their lives. Lutherans see how God cared for and sustained those saints of old to help us know God will sustain us.

The pope: As the leader of the Roman Catholic Church, the current pope has sometimes issued statements of faith that are considered infallible (direct from

God) by the Catholic church. These statements sometimes contradict Scripture. Lutherans reject this teaching. Lutherans believe that God speaks to us only through His Word, and it alone is infallible.

WHAT SCRIPTURE SAYS (15 MINUTES)

Assign each group one of the sections of Scripture. Ask each group to summarize the key teaching of the passage in their own words, in a way that would make sense to a friend who was not Lutheran. Help students express the wonderful gift of salvation through God's grace in Christ as a key teaching for the Lutheran Christian.

FAITH CONVERSATIONS (10 MINUTES)

It may be that your students will find themselves in conversation with family members or friends who are Roman Catholic. "What should be our attitude toward them? What is our goal?" Emphasize the principles that opened this study. Invite pairs of volunteers to role-play possible conversations between a Lutheran and a Roman Catholic. Invite reactions from the whole group. A possible role-play starter: a student is invited to attend church with a Catholic friend. How can the student help his or her friend understand the differences between the teachings of their church bodies?

CLOSING (5 MINUTES)

Close with prayer, thanking God for the gift of His Word, through which we learn of His love and our salvation through Christ. Ask for God's help in learning to know and share His Word with others.

9. Our Catholic Heritage

Let's Compare!

Describe what Lutherans and Catholics believe about each of these subjects:

The Reformation

Salvation

Lord's Supper

Baptism

The Bible and the Apocrypha

Purgatory

Private confession

Mary and the saints

The pope

What Scripture Says

Put these key teachings of the Christian faith in your own words.

Romans 3:21–25a

1 Peter 3:18–22

Romans 6

Ephesians 2:1–10

4

LEARN TO DISCERN

LESSON FOCUS

Religious cults and other false religions can have considerable appeal to young people. Their close personal relationships and authoritative leadership, combined with teachings that often sound biblical, are very seductive. Young people should be armed with knowledge about cults. They also need a strong faith rooted in the death and resurrection of Jesus in order to defend themselves against the lure of cults.

GOSPEL FOCUS

God states clearly that Jesus Christ is the only way to salvation. All teachings that contradict the clear word of Scripture can be resisted by those empowered by God's Word and enlightened by His Spirit.

LESSON OUTLINE

ACTIVITY	SUGGESTED TIME	MATERIALS NEEDED
Musical Moment	*5 minutes*	*Christian music, CD player*
Imagination Inquiry	*10 minutes*	*None*
Conviction Check	*15 minutes*	*Copies of Student Page, Bibles*
Accuracy Assessment	*15 minutes*	*Copies of Student Page, Bibles*
Learning to Discern	*5 minutes*	*Bibles*

A NOTE TO THE LEADER

Christians turn to the Bible to discern truth. It is God's clear Word to us, His people. Scripture is the only norm for life, faith, and truth. The Bible is the source and norm of all we teach. It is the standard by which all theological teachings are tested. (See 1 John 4:1–6; 2 Timothy 3:14–4:5; and Ephesians 6:10–18.)

Who is Jesus? and Did He really do what is said about Him? are key questions that provide much disagreement in non-Christian groups. Jesus was God, the long-awaited Messiah. He died on the cross and rose from the dead to pay the price for our sin and set us free from sin, death, and the devil. For insight into Jesus' claims and how the Jewish teachers received His testimony, read John 8:12–59.

MUSICAL MOMENT (5 MINUTES)

Greet each person by name. Play a variety of Christian music in the background. Ask participants if they like the music. What criteria do they use to judge music? Do they listen to the instruments? lyrics? something else? What makes music acceptable or unacceptable to them?

IMAGINATION INQUIRY (10 MINUTES)

Read one or both of the following "Imagination Inquiries" and discuss them to draw the students into the lesson.

Imagine that God promised to appear to you and a small group of believers this week. He's promised to answer one question aloud from each person. You get only one chance. What question would you ask God? Why? How would you decide if the answers were truthful?

Or . . .

Imagine that your best friend attended a meeting led by a person who claimed to be God. Your friend has told you what God said, but some things don't quite sound right. You're suspicious, but your friend is adamant. How would you decide if the speaker was really God?

As you lead the discussion, don't get sidetracked into answering questions about God. Instead, focus on how the students would decide if the responses were true. How would they know if they were really hearing God's truth?

CONVICTION CHECK (15 MINUTES)

Distribute copies of the Student Page. Give time for the students to individually mark the statements they believe to be true. **Also have them mark the "Accuracy Assessment" at this time.** Then form groups of three to five students to discuss this question: How do you know whether a statement is true? After the small groups have had about 10 minutes to discuss their responses, direct the whole group to the "Accuracy Assessment."

ACCURACY ASSESSMENT (15 MINUTES)

Ask each person to review how they marked this section before their discussion. Ask, "Which of these sources seems most accurate or reliable? Which would you be most willing to trust?"

Read, or have a volunteer read, 2 Timothy 3:14–17. Ask, "Why is the Bible the only source for judging religious teachings?" (It is God's Word. It reveals to us all we need in order to require forgiveness and eternal life.)

Then ask, "Which of the statements about God are true according to the Bible?"

Lead the group through the "Conviction Check" again. Use the information below to inform your discussion. For each false statement, a cult is mentioned that teaches that view along with a Bible passage that shows the teaching to be false.

Correct responses:

1. True; John 4:24

2. New Age movement; Romans 8:7; John 3:8

3. Mormonism; 2 Peter 1:21; Colossians 2:8

4. True; Romans 1:20; 1 John 5:13

5. Moonies, many other cults; Galatians 1:8; John 14:16

6. True; Romans 5:1–11

7. Hinduism, New Age theology; John 14:9–14; Romans 5:19

8. True; John 14:6; Acts 4:8–12

Remind the students that we are charged to discern and flee from false teaching (1 John 4:1–6). Emphasize that we judge spiritual teaching by the Bible, God's Word.

Read, or have a volunteer read, Galatians 1:6–10. Ask, "What are the readers being warned about? What teaching should be rejected? What 'even if ...' statements are given as warnings? Why?" Paul reminds us to hold fast to the true Gospel of Jesus Christ and to reject all false "gospels"—teachings contrary to God's Word. Even if an angel or Paul himself were to teach contrary to Scripture, we should not listen. Our eternal life is at stake. God promises salvation to those who trust in the forgiveness won for us by Jesus Christ on the cross. The best news is that as we are nurtured by our study of God's Word and our participation in Holy Communion, the Holy Spirit strengthens us to resist false teachings and hold fast to Christ.

LEARNING TO DISCERN (5 MINUTES)

Close your study by rereading 2 Timothy 3:14–17. Read it aloud as a group if possible. Close with a prayer asking God to use His Word to make us wise for salvation through faith in Jesus and equip us for every good work.

4. Learn to discern

conviction check

The following statements might be made in a discussion about God. Put a check beside the ones you think are true. Use the Bible verses to check your answer.

1. _____ God is a spirit. **(John 4:24)**

2. _____ God is in us and all living things. We should seek the divine within us and elevate its consciousness to be in tune with all creation. **(Romans 8:7; John 3:8)**

3. _____ God reveals Himself through my intuition and feelings. **(2 Peter 1:21; Colossians 2:8)**

4. _____ You can see God's power and evidence of His being in nature, but you can know His true nature only through the Bible. **(Romans 1:20; 1 John 5:13)**

5. _____ Jesus was a good teacher. God also reveals Himself in the teachings of Muhammad and other chosen religious leaders. **(Galatians 1:8; John 14:16)**

6. _____ Knowing Jesus is the only way to have peace with God. Faith in Him gives forgiveness, acceptance, and eternal life. **(Romans 5:1–11)**

7. _____ Jesus is one of many people who achieved the highest level of understanding and have been elevated to godhood. **(John 14:9–14; Romans 5:19)**

8. _____ Jesus is the only way to heaven. **(John 14:6; Acts 4:8–12)**

accuracy assessment

How did you decide if a statement was true? Check any reasons you used:

_____ intuition

_____ a Bible verse

_____ previous experience

_____ something learned previously

_____ what someone else said

_____ other:_____

cults

5

OUR SAVIOR'S FAITH

LESSON FOCUS

Through His chosen people, the children of Israel, God carried out His plan of salvation. Our Messiah, Jesus Himself, was ethnically a Jew. God's Spirit enables us to share the Gospel of Jesus Christ with our Jewish neighbors.

GOSPEL FOCUS

Through His Word God demonstrates His plan of salvation for all people. Moved by His Spirit we can share that plan with the followers of Judaism.

Lesson Outline

ACTIVITY	SUGGESTED TIME	MATERIAL NEEDED
Opening	5 minutes	Newsprint and markers
Who Are the Jews?	15 minutes	None
The Fulfillment of Prophecy	20 minutes	Copies of Student Page, Bibles
Speaking the Gospel with Both Testaments	15 minutes	Copies of Student Page, Bibles
Closing	5 minutes	Hymnals

A NOTE TO THE LEADER

Depending on your community, many students may have little contact with Jewish people. Before leading this section, be sure to review the information about Jewish beliefs. *How to Respond: Judaism* by Erwin J. Kolb (CPH item no. 12-6013) contains a detailed description of Jewish teachings. Additional information is also available from Apple of His Eye Mission Society (www.appleofhiseye.org) or Lutherans in Jewish Evangelism (www.lutheransonline.com/lije). Consider taking a class "field trip" to a local synagogue before or after this study.

OPENING (5 MINUTES)

As you begin this lesson, be aware that some students may have preconceived ideas and perhaps even anti-Semitic feelings. Stress that such feelings are sinful, but that God freely forgives even the sins of prejudice and hate.

Ask students to share information that they know about the Jewish faith or Jewish traditions. Record their answers on the board or newsprint. As you review their responses, point out correct or incorrect understandings that students may have.

Begin with prayer, asking God to bless your study of His Word as you seek to understand and witness to the Jewish people.

WHO ARE THE JEWS? (15 MINUTES)

Help students understand the Jewish people and their faith by summarizing the following information:

Jewish people consider themselves the ethnic descendants of the Hebrews, or the Israelites in Old Testament. The Jewish race traces its ancestry to the covenant that God established with Abraham and his descendants.

To understand Judaism today, we must distinguish between biblical Judaism of the Old Testament, and modern Judaism, which is known as rabbinic or talmudic Judaism. Modern Judaism has its roots in the Talmud, which was written between A.D. 200 and 600. The Talmud is considered the authoritative commentary on the Old Testament Scriptures. Judaism has three major branches in America.

Orthodox Judaism

Orthodox Jews devote themselves to the strict observance of all 613 commandments they count in the Torah, the first five books of the Bible. They strictly observe the Sabbath, and the Orthodox synagogue is segregated by gender. Hebrew is used in the synagogue, and the heads of both men and women are always covered. Orthodox Jews strictly observe kosher dietary laws. Kosher dietary regulations include avoiding "unclean" foods such as pork and blood, and not consuming dairy and meat products at the same meal. Orthodox Jews pray three times each day: morning, afternoon, and after sunset.

Reform Judaism

Reform (not Reform*ed*) Jewish beliefs are focused on the hope for a messianic time of peace for humanity, not a personal Messiah. Reform teaching reflects a progressive revelation that takes into account changes throughout history. Reform believers worship at "temple" rather than a synagogue, at which English is used, services are coed, and music is present. Reform Jews may or may not believe even in the presence of God.

Conservative Judaism

Conservative Judaism may be considered the "middle ground" between Orthodox and Reform. The majority of people who describe themselves as Jews are part of the Conservative movement. The Conservatives observe some of the traditions of Judaism, such as modified dietary laws and the use of both English and Hebrew in worship. Conservatives see Jewish culture as the unifying bond for Jews.

There are also Christian Jews. Known as Messianic Jews, these ethnically Jewish people believe that Jesus of Nazareth is the promised Messiah. They believe that Jesus died and rose again to save them from their sins. In other words, they are Christians. Like the early church, these individuals may have been raised in a traditional Jewish household. By the Holy Spirit, through the Word of God, they have been led to faith.

THE FULFILLMENT OF PROPHECY (20 MINUTES)

Distribute copies of the Student Page as you divide students into small groups. Direct groups to look up each pair of verses and record the prophecy that is foretold and fulfilled in these verses. Once students have completed their work, use the information that follows to summarize their findings. Point out that this list is far from complete. The entire Old Testament prepares the way for Jesus and points to Him.

Old Testament	Prophecy	New Testament
Genesis 3:15	Seed of the woman	Galatians 4:4
Genesis 12:1–3, 7	Covenant of Abraham	Romans 9:4–5
Genesis 49:10	Tribe of Judah	Matthew 1:2–3
Deuteronomy 18:15–19	Prophet like Moses	Acts 3:19–23
Isaiah 7:14	Born of a virgin	Matthew 1:18–20
Micah 5:2	Born in Bethlehem	Matthew 2:1–6
Jeremiah 31:31–34	New covenant	Hebrews 8:1–13
Isaiah 53	Death for our forgiveness	Luke 23:26–54
Jonah 1:17–2:10	Resurrection	Matthew 12:39–40; 16:4, 21

SPEAKING THE GOSPEL WITH BOTH TESTAMENTS (15 MINUTES)

In order to witness concerning Christ to our Jewish neighbors, we need to present the Gospel from both the Old Testament (Hebrew Scriptures) and the New Testament. To effectively witness to a Jewish person, you need to know whether that person is Orthodox, Conservative, or Reform. The Orthodox Jew has an understanding of God much like the Christian. On the other hand a Reform Jew may have a view that resembles atheism.

Direct students to this section of the Student Page as they work in small groups. Allow time for students to look up the verses and outline the Gospel message found in these Old and New Testament Scriptures. Use the information that follows to summarize student findings. Be sure to stress the concepts of atonement and that Jesus was the final sacrifice for all sin.

1. All have sinned and need atonement with God (Ecclesiastes 7:20; Isaiah 64:6; Psalm 14:2–3; Romans 3:23).

2. The result of sin is death (Isaiah 59:1–2; Ezekiel 18:4; Romans 6:23a).

3. God removes sin by sacrifice (Leviticus 17:11; Isaiah 53:3–8; John 1:29; Romans 6:23b).

4. God takes away sin and changes the heart (Psalm 51:7–13; Galatians 2:15–16; Galatians 5:22–23).

5. Salvation is received through faith (Genesis 15:6; 1 Kings 18:21; Galatians 3:6–7).

CLOSING (5 MINUTES)

Close with a prayer asking God to help your students witness their faith to those who do not yet know Jesus as Lord and Savior. Sing together "King of Kings" (*All God's People Sing!* 151), which is based on a traditional Jewish folk tune.

5. OuR saVioR's Faith

the FuLFiLLMent OF PROPheCY

Use the chart below to look up the prophecies concerning Christ in both the Old and New Testaments. List the prophecy told and fulfilled in the center column.

Old Testament	Prophecy	New Testament
Genesis 3:15		Galatians 4:4
Genesis 12:1–3, 7		Romans 9:4–5
Genesis 49:10		Matthew 1:2–3
Deuteronomy 18:15–19		Acts 3:19–23
Isaiah 7:14		Matthew 1:18–20
Micah 5:2		Matthew 2:1–6
Jeremiah 31:31–34		Hebrews 8:1–13
Isaiah 53		Luke 23:26–54
Jonah 1:17–2:10		Matthew 12:39–40; 16:4, 21

speaking the gospeL With bOth testaments

In order to share the Gospel of Jesus Christ with the Jewish person, we need to use both the Old Testament (Hebrew Scriptures) and the New Testament. Use the verses below to outline the Gospel message.

1. **Ecclesiastes 7:20; Isaiah 64:6; Psalm 14:2–3; Romans 3:23**
2. **Isaiah 59:1–2; Ezekiel 18:4; Romans 6:23a**
3. **Leviticus 17:11; Isaiah 53:3–8; John 1:29; Romans 6:23b**
4. **Psalm 51:7–13; Galatians 2:15–16; Galatians 5:22–23**
5. **Genesis 15:6; Galatians 3:6–7**

6 What do Mormons believe?

LESSON FOCUS

Through this study students will realize that the only reliable source of information about God is what God provides to us in His Word. Participants will compare what they believe to some of the beliefs of Mormonism and give thanks for the confidence God gives them to talk with others about their Savior.

GOSPEL FOCUS

God clearly reveals Himself in His Word, offering His promise of forgiveness of sins and eternal life through faith in Christ Jesus. Through faith strengthened by the Holy Spirit working through the Word, we can be confident in our Savior and prepared to have discussions about Him with others.

Lesson Outline

ACTIVITY	SUGGESTED TIME	MATERIALS NEEDED
Opening	5 minutes	None
What Do I Believe?	10 minutes	Copies of Student Page, Apostles' Creed
What Do Mormons Believe?	15 minutes	Copies of Student Page
Whom Can You Believe?	15 minutes	Copies of Student Page, Bibles
Put Your Money . . .	10 minutes	Concordances, Bibles
Closing	5 minutes	None

A NOTE TO THE LEADER

The closing activities will go more smoothly if you prepare in advance. Plan to bring a few large concordance-type resources or Bibles with smaller concordances in the back. If you have additional time, mark places where verses on Scripture, Word, Father, Son, Spirit, believe, and other key terms are found. If you have access to a computerized concordance, you might even print up lists of verses ahead of time.

OPENING (5 MINUTES)

Tell the following story:

> *The American Bankers Association offers a special 10-day class to teach bank tellers how to identify counterfeit money. Interestingly enough, for the first nine days of the class, no one is shown counterfeit money. Everything they handle and examine is real. Only on the last day of the class is counterfeit money shown to the students. Why do you suppose the counterfeit money is shown only on the last day?*

Then ask, "Why is it important to know what you believe before studying what others believe?" Tell students that in today's session they will first examine what they believe about God and then look at some of the teachings of the Mormons.

WHAT DO I BELIEVE? (10 MINUTES)

Have students answer the questions on the Student Page independently. Allow volunteers to share their answers. If time permits, have students compare their answers. Then share the following in your own words:

"Throughout the ages people have asked Christians what they believe or have challenged the things that Christians believe. For this reason the Christian church has adopted creeds, or 'I believe' statements, that clearly state the teachings of Holy Scripture."

Review the words of the Apostles' Creed. Help the students compare the "I believe" statements of this creed to the answers they gave to the questions on the Student Page.

WHAT DO MORMONS BELIEVE? (15 MINUTES)

Read aloud the statements that a Mormon might make if asked, "What do you believe?" You may wish to provide the following additional information concerning Mormonism:

The Mormon church is well known in North America. Otherwise known as The Church of Jesus Christ of Latter-day Saints, it was begun by a young man named Joseph Smith. Smith was troubled by the conflicts among various denominations and confused about which church to join.

According to Mormon history, the angel Moroni visited Smith while he was deep in prayer. Moroni told Smith that all religions were wrong and that God had chosen him to reveal the true religion to the world. Years later, following several subsequent visions, Jesus supposedly appeared to Smith and directed him to find and dig up a package of special gold plates written in an ancient Egyptian language. Although Smith could not read the plates, the package also contained a pair of spectacles that enabled Smith to read and translate the writing. He later published it as the *Book of Mormon*.

Religious persecution against the small cult that Smith founded forced them to migrate from New York to Ohio, and later to Illinois. When Smith was killed, the group split into two groups. One group followed Smith's son, Joseph Smith Jr. to Kansas City, Missouri, forming the Reorganized Church of Jesus Christ of Latter Day Saints. The second—and larger—group remained faithful to Smith's teaching and followed Brigham Young to Utah. Today the Mormon church has a vast agricultural, financial, and genealogical empire.

Mormons may call themselves Christian, but their teachings are definitely not Christian. Mormons believe that Jesus was only a person. They consider the Trinity a pagan attempt to explain the unexplainable.

While accepting the Holy Bible, Mormons believe the Bible can be understood only in the light of the *Book of Mormon*.

Mormons talk about Christ's death for them, but they also teach works-righteousness, the need to perform sufficient good works in order to earn entrance into heaven. Since the Mormon heaven has many levels, ambitious members can receive greater rewards if they perform more good works. No member can ever be assured that he or she has done enough to merit forgiveness of sins and eternal life.

Offer the students an opportunity to ask questions or offer insights about what they have heard.

WHOM CAN YOU BELIEVE? (15 MINUTES)

Have the students work in groups of three to five to read the brief statements and Scripture verses and to answer the study questions. After each set of questions, allow volunteers to share responses on behalf of each group.

1. Read 2 Timothy 3:15–17. What knowledge of God does Scripture provide us? (Only Scripture is "able to make you wise for salvation through faith in Christ Jesus.")

2. Why is it so important for us to continue to look to Scripture for questions concerning God? (God reveals all that we need to know about Him in Scripture.)

3. Read 2 Timothy 4:3–4. How does this section describe the teachings of Mormonism and other cults? (Mormonism and all other religions that have turned to human reason instead of God's Word are only myths.)

4. What other "itching ears" teachings have you heard (2 Timothy 4:3)? (Chances are that students have heard about some of the teachings of other cult groups or of Satanism. All false teachings are examples of itching ears.)

PUT YOUR MONEY WHERE YOUR MOUTH IS (10 MINUTES)

Supported by our knowledge of God's Word and faith in His Son, we can talk about our faith in conversation with others. Challenge students to choose a verse or two of Scripture to support each of the three "pillars of faith" (the Bible, God, and salvation). Encourage students to find verses that reinforce, "the reason for the hope that you have" (1 Peter 3:15).

CLOSING (5 MINUTES)

Give students an opportunity to offer sentence prayers of thanksgiving to God for the Bible, for their faith, and for opportunities to discuss their faith with others.

IF YOU HAVE MORE TIME

Show the video *The God-Makers* (Jeremiah Films), available from most Christian bookstores. This video provides an in-depth look at the development and teachings of the Mormon religion.

6. What do Mormons believe?

What do i believe?

How would you respond if someone asked you the following questions?

1. What do you believe about the Bible?

2. What do you believe about God?

3. What do you believe about salvation?

What do Mormons believe?

If asked, "What do you believe?" a trained Mormon might share some of the following information:

1. "I believe that the Book of Mormon has more authority than the Holy Bible."

2. "I believe the Trinity—God the Father, God the Son, and God the Holy Spirit—is a pagan attempt to explain the unexplainable."

3. "I believe that God was once a man. Through obedience, we can become like God."

In what ways do these statements contradict our Christian faith?

Whom can you believe?

On our own, we can never truly know God. That is why God reveals all we need to know about Him in the Scriptures.

1. Read **2 Timothy 3:15–17.** What knowledge of God does Scripture provide us?

2. Why is it so important for us to continue to look to Scripture for questions concerning God?

3. Read **2 Timothy 4:3–4.** How does this section describe the teachings of Mormonism and other cults?

4. What other "itching ears" teachings have you heard **(2 Timothy 4:3)**?

7

jehovah's witnesses: understanding their beliefs

LESSON FOCUS

Young people are naturally curious about the beliefs of others. God would not have us belittle or reject anyone on account of his or her beliefs, but He warns us to reject beliefs that are contrary to His Word. He empowers us to cling to the truth of His Word and to share it.

GOSPEL FOCUS

God clearly reveals Himself in His Word, offering His promise of forgiveness of sins and eternal life through faith in Jesus Christ. Young people, enabled by the Spirit through their study of God's Word, can confidently discuss their beliefs with others and discern scriptural truth in the face of conflicting beliefs.

Lesson Outline

ACTIVITY	SUGGESTED TIME	MATERIALS NEEDED
Opening Activity	10 minutes	Newsprint or whiteboard
Jehovah's Witness	15 minutes	None
A Contrary Creed	10 minutes	Copies of Student Page
What Scripture Says	15 minutes	Copies of Student Page, Bibles
Life Application	5 minutes	None

A NOTE TO THE LEADER

As you prepare for this lesson, you are encouraged to read *How to Respond to the Jehovah's Witnesses* (CPH item no. 12-6005). Information and statistics for this lesson have been drawn from this source. An additional Bible study on Jehovah's Witnesses is available in the book *One God, many gods* (CPH item no. 20-2427).

OPENING (10 MINUTES)

Write the following questions on the board or on newsprint before class. Ask the students to respond to them.

　* Is the word Trinity found in the Bible?

　* Was Jesus Christ an angel, or was He God?

　* Is Jesus Christ as a human being dead?

　* Is the Holy Spirit God, part of God, or just the activity of God?

　　If the students seem uncertain or answer some of these questions incorrectly, do not criticize them. Ask questions such as, "Why do you say that? Do you remember a Bible passage that supports that belief? What groups do you know that hold that belief?" Point out to the students that the questions are basic to our Christian faith and that the correct responses will be shared during the study, along with why they pose a problem for people who identify themselves as Jehovah's Witnesses.

　　Lead a prayer like the following:

> Almighty God, thank You for revealing Yourself to us through the Bible as Father, Son, and Holy Spirit. We thank You, dear Father, for creating us and keeping us going. We thank You, Lord Jesus, for saving us from sin by Your death on the cross and Your glorious rising to life on Easter morning. We thank You, Holy Spirit, for creating faith in our hearts to trust in Jesus and strengthening us to follow Him. Bless our study today. Open our minds to Your Word. Make us bold witnesses of You and Your love. We ask this, O Father, through Jesus Christ, Your Son, our Lord, who lives and reigns with You and the Holy Spirit, one God, now and forever. Amen.

JEHOVAH'S WITNESSES (15 MINUTES)

　　Ask the students to share any firsthand experiences they may have with Jehovah's Witnesses: door-to-door, classmates, friends, family, and so forth. Keep this to firsthand experience, not secondhand information. Experience may be limited to seeing them in the neighborhood or passing a kingdom hall. Be alert to those students who have relatives or friends who are Jehovah's Witnesses. Be sensitive to these relationships as you proceed with the study, since people often base the merit of a religion upon persons whom they know who are part of it.

　　Point out that the Jehovah's Witnesses are not considered by Christians to be a sect (a branch, a division) of Christianity. Share this brief historical background of the Jehovah's Witnesses:

> The Jehovah's Witnesses were founded by Charles Taze Russell about 1872 and have been known by several names which include "Millennial Dawnist" and

"The Watchtower Bible and Tract Society." They number over 2 million in the United States. They are best known for their door-to-door visiting and the distribution of their magazines entitled The Watchtower *and* Awake! *They often receive media attention for their refusal to salute a national flag, to serve in the military by bearing arms, or to receive a blood transfusion.*

The Jehovah's Witnesses reject many of the teachings of Christianity, including the triune God, the reality of hell, and the immortality of the soul. They denounce Christians and Christian churches as enemies of God.

A CONTRARY CREED (10 MINUTES)

Distribute the Student Page. Remind the students that as Christians we accept certain creeds that briefly state what we believe and teach, including the Apostles' Creed and the Nicene Creed. Point out the "creed" on the Student Page. **Stress that this is *not* an official creed of the Jehovah's Witnesses, but it contains the beliefs that they teach, taken from materials they print and distribute.**

Ask, "How does this creed differ from the creeds you confess in worship?" Among the discrepancies students may notice are the use of the name Jehovah, Jesus as an angel, the Spirit as God's action, the rejection of the concept of a triune God and an immortal soul, the reliance on obedience for salvation, and the literal interpretation of the 144,000 mentioned in Revelation 7:3–4.

WHAT SCRIPTURE SAYS (15 MINUTES)

Form small groups of three to five students. Assign each group one or more of the groups of Scripture passages to read and summarize. After about seven minutes invite reports from each group. As the groups share their findings, include the following information if it is not shared.

The Holy Trinity

Since the words *Trinity* and *triune* are not found in the Bible, Jehovah's Witnesses reject the concept of one God revealing Himself in three distinct persons. Yet the triune God is clearly present in each of the passages: Matthew 28:18–20—Jesus commands Baptism in the name of the triune God, Father, Son, and Holy Spirit; Mark 1:9–11—at Jesus' own baptism the triune God was acknowledged (the Holy Spirit in the form of dove, the Father in the speaking of His word, and Jesus called "Son" by the Father); 2 Corinthians 13:14—Paul gives a blessing in God's name in these words, "the grace of the Lord Jesus Christ, the love of God, and the fellowship of the Holy Spirit."

The Holy Spirit

The Jehovah's Witnesses reject the Holy Spirit as God. Yet the Scriptures describe Him as a distinct person in the Godhead: Matthew 3:16–17—The Holy Spirit takes visible form; John 14:26—The Holy Spirit involves Himself in the teaching of Christian truth and is referred to here with a masculine pronoun (He), not a neuter form; Acts 13:2—The Holy Spirit is involved in the spread of the Gospel and here refers to Himself with the personal pronoun of "Me."

Jesus, True God and True Man?

Jehovah's Witnesses teach that Jesus was at first an angel, then for 33 years lived as a man on earth only to die and rot in the grave, and now He is an angel again in heaven. But Scripture clearly teaches otherwise: John 1:1–5, 14—Jesus Christ, the Word of God, is clearly both God and man; John 3:16—Jesus is the only-begotten Son of God, through whom we are saved by faith; Colossians 2:9–10—In Christ the fullness of God lived in human form and yet rules over every power and authority.

LIFE APPLICATION (5 MINUTES)

Say, "Though Jehovah's Witnesses teach an unscriptural message, they do not hesitate to share it boldly door-to-door. The Bible gives us the right message about the triune God and about everlasting life in His name. God works in us through our faith in Christ and through His Word and Sacraments to empower us to share that message of hope.

"Think about someone in your life who could profit from a friend like you sharing a Friend like Jesus with them. Pray for the Holy Spirit's guidance, timing, boldness, and words. Then sometime, perhaps this week, share your faith in Jesus with that person." Conclude with a prayer for God's help in sharing your faith.

7. Jehovah's Witnesses: Understanding Their Beliefs

a contrary creed

I believe in Father God Jehovah, Maker of heaven and earth.

I believe in Jesus Christ, who was created as an angel in eternity, who clothed his angelic identity with flesh for a time on earth, who suffered under Pontius Pilate, was crucified, and died. His body was buried, and he returned to heaven again an angel.

I believe in Jehovah's active force. I reject all churches that profess the Trinity and the immortality of the soul. I believe that salvation comes through obedience to God's Law. I believe that 144,000 spirit creatures will reign as associate kings with the Lamb Jesus Christ in heaven, governing the other believers forever on a perfect earth.

what Scripture says

The Holy Trinity

Jehovah's Witnesses do not believe God is a Trinity, since the word Trinity *is not found in the Bible. The Bible says:*

Matthew 28:18–20

Mark 1:9–11

2 Corinthians 13:14

the hOLy SPiRit

The Jehovah's Witnesses say the Holy Spirit is not God, but only a way of describing God's action. The Bible says:

Matthew 3:16–17

John 14:26

Acts 13:2

jesus, tRUe god and tRUe man?

According to the Jehovah's Witnesses, Jesus is not God but an angel who lived as a man on earth for 33 years. The Bible says:

John 1:1–5, 14

John 3:16

Colossians 2:9–10

8

WHAT KIND OF
LUTHERAN ARE YOU?

LESSON FOCUS

The variety of churches that bear the label "Lutheran" are far from united in their confessions and practice. Through this lesson students will study the some of the major differences that separate these various Lutheran church bodies.

GOSPEL FOCUS

God promises salvation to all those who believe in Jesus Christ as Lord and Savior. Through God's Word the Holy Spirit teaches all that is needed concerning faith and life.

Lesson Outline

ACTIVITY	SUGGESTED TIME	MATERIALS NEEDED
Who Are the Lutherans?	*10 minutes*	*Copies of Student Page*
The Big Three	*15 minutes*	*None*
You Are What You Teach	*15 minutes*	*Copies of Student Page, Bibles*
Closing	*5 minutes*	*None*

A NOTE TO THE LEADER

There are a least 24 recognized Lutheran church bodies in North America today. For more information about each of these bodies see the links available from the Valparaiso University Office of Church Relations site at www.valpo.edu/lutheran/LutheranChurchBodies.html.

WHO ARE THE LUTHERANS? (10 MINUTES)

Distribute copies of the Student Page to each participant. Allow a few minutes for individuals to respond to each statement. After students have finished, review the correct responses to each statement.

1. *T or F Martin Luther, a former German monk, was one of the leaders of the Protestant Reformation in Europe. (True)*

2. *T or F Martin Luther first coined the term* Lutheran *when referring to the members in his first congregation. (False, in fact, the term* Lutheran *was originally used by enemies when speaking of Luther's followers, who later adopted the name themselves.)*

3. *T or F The use of German in Lutheran worship services in the United States declined greatly in the years around World War I due to anti-German sentiments. (True, plus many churches saw the use of English as an outreach effort to their non-Lutheran English-speaking neighbors.)*

4. *T or F Of the three largest Lutheran bodies in North America, The Lutheran Church—Missouri Synod is the largest. (False. The LCMS has approximately 2.6 million members. The WELS has 412,000 members. The ELCA is the largest, with about 5.1 million baptized members.)*

5. *T or F North America boasts the second largest population of Lutherans in the world. (True. With 8.7 million Lutherans, America comes in second after Germany, with 14.7 million Lutherans.)*

6. *T or F Among the ELCA, LCMS, and WELS, the WELS is the oldest Lutheran church body in America. (False. The LCMS was founded in 1847; the WELS followed in 1850. The merger that formed the ELCA occurred in 1988.)*

7. *T or F The different Lutheran church bodies formed because of regional differences among the members. (False. The split among the Lutheran churches is due largely to differences in doctrine and practice, especially concerning how Scripture is interpreted and understood.)*

8. *T or F When the different Lutheran church bodies are counted together, Lutheranism is still one of the fastest growing "mainline" Christian churches in America. (False. Like most mainline churches, the combined Lutheran churches in North America have seen steady decline in recent years. It is interesting to note that the Lutheran church is growing fastest in Africa, which numbers some 6.2 million Lutherans.)*

9. *T or F There are at least 24 different Lutheran synods (church bodies) in North America. (True)*

10. T or F Of the three largest Lutheran church bodies in North America, the LCMS has the greatest number of elementary and high schools. (True. The LCMS has 1,120 elementary and high schools, the WELS has 388, and the ELCA 293.)

THE BIG THREE (15 MINUTES)

Use the information that follows to provide students a quick summary of each of the three major Lutheran church bodies in America.

ELCA—Evangelical Lutheran Church in America

The largest of the Lutheran church bodies in America (5.1 million members), the ELCA was formed in 1988 through the merger of the former American Lutheran Church (ALC), The Lutheran Church in America (LCA), and the Association of Evangelical Lutheran Churches (AELC). Both the ALC and the LCA were formed through the merger of smaller ethnic synods in the 1960s. The AELC split off from The Lutheran Church—Missouri Synod in 1976.

The ELCA constitution states that, "This church accepts the canonical Scriptures of the Old and New Testaments as the inspired Word of God and the authoritative source and norm of its proclamation, faith, and life" (www.elca.org). At the same time the ELCA also accepts a nonliteral method to interpret Scripture, in which the time and place in which passages were written are studied to assist in interpretation.

The ELCA allows for the ordination of women in the pastoral ministry, about 15 percent of its pastors are female. As a result of its worldwide Christian unity efforts, the ELCA has opened the door for the participation of homosexuals in church leadership.

Since its formation the ELCA has established fellowship with a number of other churches through its ecumenical efforts. The ELCA is in full pulpit and altar fellowship with the Episcopal Church (USA), the Moravian Church in America, the Presbyterian Church (USA), the Reformed Church in America, the United Church of Christ, and the Lutheran World Federation.

WELS—Wisconsin Evangelical Lutheran Synod

The Wisconsin Evangelical Lutheran Synod was founded by three German pastors who met in Milwaukee in 1850. Generally considered the most conservative of the three major Lutheran church bodies, the WELS is also the smallest in number (412,000 baptized members).

The WELS is in fellowship with the ELS (Evangelical Lutheran Synod) and various Lutheran church bodies in foreign countries. WELS congregations seek to strengthen their membership through the study of God's Word and participation in the Sacraments.

LCMS—The Lutheran Church—Missouri Synod

Founded with 12 pastors and 15 congregations in 1847 as "The German Evangelical Lutheran Synod of Missouri, Ohio, and Other States," The Lutheran Church—Missouri Synod has grown to be the second largest Lutheran body in America (2.6 million members). While the LCMS is in fellowship with some other Lutheran churches, these relationships are entered into with much study and care.

The LCMS is well known for its emphasis on biblical doctrine and faithfulness to historic Lutheran Confessions. Following a dramatic walkout at the St. Louis seminary in 1974 concerning the literal interpretation of Scripture, the LCMS reclaimed its historic confessional stance on the doctrine and authority of Holy Scripture as the inspired and inerrant Word of God.

The LCMS places a high priority on Christ-centered beliefs and practices. The synod acknowledges the sinfulness of man and God's actions in the past, present, and future in granting life and salvation. The Sacraments of Baptism and Holy Communion are strongly emphasized in the LCMS.

YOU ARE WHAT YOU TEACH (15 MINUTES)

Church bodies are defined by their public confessions and teachings. The Lutheran Church—Missouri Synod bases its teachings on the unchanging Word of God. Assign students to work together in three groups to study one of the areas of concern to the church. Once the groups have completed their work, have them report to the whole group as you summarize their findings.

God's Word

Proverbs 30:5—Every Word of God is true. God promises to protect those who trust in Him.

2 Peter 1:21—The Scriptures were inspired by God, through the work of the Holy Spirit. Men recorded this message in their own unique style.

1 Corinthians 2:13—The human authors of the Scriptures were not speaking for themselves; rather, they spoke the message inspired by the Spirit.

2 Timothy 3:15–16—The Scriptures are intended for all ages, even the young. They are used to guide humankind in the message of salvation and holy living.

John 10:35—The Scriptures are completely reliable. Scripture always proves true.

Luke 11:28—God blesses those who hear and do His word.

John 5:39—Eternal life is not based on our knowledge of Scripture; rather, it is based on the work of Christ as Lord and Savior.

Creeds

1 Peter 3:15—The creeds provide the opportunity for us to testify our beliefs before others. "A creed is a statement of what we believe, teach, and confess." (Small Catechism: The Apostles' Creed, p.99)

Matthew 10:32—Christ acknowledges us before the Father, as we confess Him before humankind.

Matthew 16:13–16—Peter gives his personal confession of Jesus as Lord and Savior.

Matthew 7:15—God warns against false teaching.

Unity of the Church

Ephesians 4:3–6—There is but one Christian faith. The Small Catechism defines this "invisible church" as "the total number of those who believe in Christ. All believers in Christ, but only believers, are members of the church" (Small Catechism: The Church, the Communion of Saints, pp. 153–154) This is not to say that we should all be one church. Because we live in a sinful world, there will be no true unity of believers until Jesus returns.

Romans 16:17—Paul warns against false teachers in the church, who lead believers away from the faith.

Hebrews 10:23–25—We are encouraged to meet together to support fellow believers with whom we share a common confession.

CLOSING (5 MINUTES)

Close with a prayer thanking God for giving us His Word and helping us to remain true to the teachings that He gives us in the Scriptures.

8. What Kind Of Lutheran are you?

Who are the Lutherans?

_____ 1. T or F Martin Luther, a former German monk, was one of the leaders of the Protestant Reformation in Europe.

_____ 2. T or F Martin Luther first coined the term Lutheran _when referring to the members in his first congregation._

_____ 3. T or F The use of German in Lutheran worship services in the United States declined greatly in the years around World War I due to anti-German sentiments.

_____ 4. T or F Of the three largest Lutheran bodies in North America, The Lutheran Church—Missouri Synod is the largest.

_____ 5. T or F North America boasts the second largest population of Lutherans in the world.

_____ 6. T or F Among the ELCA, LCMS, and WELS, the WELS is the oldest Lutheran church body in America.

_____ 7. T or F The different Lutheran church bodies formed because of regional differences among the members.

_____ 8. T or F When the different Lutheran church bodies are counted together, Lutheranism is still one of the fastest growing "mainline" Christian churches in America.

_____ 9. T or F There are at least 24 different Lutheran synods (church bodies) in North America.

_____ 10. T or F Of the three largest Lutheran church bodies in North America, the LCMS has the greatest number of elementary and high schools.

you are what you teach

God's Word

    Proverbs 30:5

    2 Peter 1:21

    1 Corinthians 2:13

    2 Timothy 3:15–16

    John 10:35

    Luke 11:28

    John 5:39

Creeds

    1 Peter 3:15

    Matthew 10:32

    Matthew 16:13–16

    Matthew 7:15

Unity of the Church

    Ephesians 4:3–6

    Romans 16:17

    Hebrews 10:23–25

9

feed the POOR?
i've got EXPENSES!

LESSON FOCUS

Through this study participants will begin to recognize their material blessings as gifts from God. Students will rejoice in the "best gift"—Christ's death and resurrection. Participants will thankfully respond to God's generosity by giving to those who are in need.

GOSPEL FOCUS

God created us and gives us all that we need to live. He does this out of love even though we sin daily. Jesus gave His life as payment for our many sins. He asks us to give generously to Him by giving to others. As the Holy Spirit continues to work in us, He enables us to give willingly of our time, talents, and resources.

Lesson Outline

ACTIVITY	SUGGESTED TIME	MATERIALS NEEDED
Total Cost	10 minutes	Paper, pen, or pencil; newsprint/chalkboard
True or Change It	10 minutes	Copies of Student Page, Bibles
Great Givers	15 minutes	Copies of Student Page, Bibles
A Love Letter	10 minutes	Copies of Student Page, Bibles
Closing	5 minutes	Paper, pen or pencil

TOTAL COST (10 MINUTES)

Ask students to create a bill for the items God has given to them. Ask them to write in general terms, not to list each item individually (for example, clothes, food, etc.; not blue sweater, cereal). Encourage students to work with a partner or in groups. Have students total their bills. For ideas of things to include on their lists you may want to consult the list of the things God provides for us found in Luther's explanation of the first article of the Apostles' Creed from the Small Catechism.

Pray, "Heavenly Father, thank You for all the gifts You so generously give to us. Please help us to use these gifts wisely for ourselves and for others. We pray in Jesus' name because He generously gave His life for us so that we may live. Amen."

Ask students to share items from their lists. Make one bill on a chalkboard or a large sheet of newsprint. Add items students may not have thought of, such as the beauty of the sunset, love, answers to prayers, and so forth.

Total the bill. Discuss the enormity of the bill and how it would be impossible to put a monetary value on many items. Help students realize that God's gifts to us are priceless. Ask, "What is God's greatest gift?" God sent His only Son to die for our sins, not because of anything we did, but because He loves us.

TRUE OR CHANGE IT (10 MINUTES)

Divide into groups of three to five. Assign each group a statement from the Student Page. Ask them to evaluate and correct the statement if necessary. Invite sharing. Use the comments below to assist in discussion.

1. Everything I have belongs to God. *God created and sustains all things. As Luther was about to die he proclaimed, "We are all beggars." We enter the world with nothing but a sinful heart and we leave this world with nothing but eternal life, which we did not earn.*

2. Sharing what we have with others is a privilege. *The desire to give comes from an overflowing joy (2 Corinthians 8:2) because Christ has done so much for me.*

3. God became poor so we might become rich. *Ask, "How did God become poor? To what kind of riches does this verse refer?" Jesus left the riches of heaven to live on earth and to suffer and die for us so we could have all the riches of heaven.*

4. Those who have more should give more. *Ask, "Which is more important, how much you give or how much you have left after you give? Which is better, to give a large amount reluctantly or a small amount willingly?" In Old Testament times people were required to give 10 percent of their income (Leviticus 27:30). In Malachi 3:8–10, God says we rob Him when we withhold the tithe. He promises to pour out blessings on those who give it. While we no longer live under the law, many Christians willingly use the tithe as a guideline for their giving.*

5. We give to others who are in need as we acknowledge what God has done and given to us. *We realize that nothing is really "ours." It is all from God. We cannot buy God's love. Our salvation cannot be earned. Jesus earned our salvation for us. We can only thank God for what He has already done.*

GREAT GIVERS (15 MINUTES)

Have students read each of the statements. Ask for names of Bible characters who might have made the statement. Give and have someone read the Bible references if necessary. The comments after each imagined quotation may be helpful.

"I ordered the people to stop giving because they gave so generously we had more than we could use." Exodus 36:6–7

1. Moses, at God's instruction, invited the Israelites "who [were] willing and whose heart moved [them]" (Exodus 35:21) to give a material offering or an offering of service to be used in the building of the tabernacle. Their response was so great that they had more than they needed.

"The offering I gave was very little, but Jesus said it was more than anyone else gave." Mark 12:41–43

2. The widow gave all she had, even though it was only two small coins. God had promised through His Word that He would provide all she needed.

"Jesus was pleased when I gave Him my expensive perfume." John 12:3–8

3. Moved by His love and grace, Mary anointed Jesus with nard, an expensive perfume usually used for festivities or for burials. Although Judas complained about the wastefulness of such an act, Jesus praised Mary for her extravagance in honoring Him in such a way.

"Even though we were very poor, we begged Paul to let us give money to the Christians in Jerusalem." 2 Corinthians 8:1–5

4. The Macedonians gave themselves first to the Lord, and He enabled them to give generously to others. The power of the Spirit moved the people to put Jesus first in their lives and changed their priorities, including what they did with their money. God's grace changes our attitude toward giving.

"Because of My great love, I gave the best I had to people who didn't even know me." Romans 5:8

5. God gave His Son. Jesus gave His life. We gain heaven because of this great love.

Remind students that none of the first four people listed was greater than any other because of their giving. They were able to give freely because of Christ in them, through the indwelling of the Holy Spirit. On our own we are miserable, self-centered people who don't know how to share with others. It is only through the grace and forgiveness of Christ that we are able to share our blessings with others.

A LOVE LETTER (10 MINUTES)

Have students work in small groups or pairs to complete the love letter. The following are suggested responses for the promises of God.

2 Corinthians 9:6 —Give generously as I have given generously to you, and you will receive generously.

2 Corinthians 9:8—I will give you all you need. *God always replenishes the supply of what we give away.*

2 Corinthians 9:10—I enable you through Jesus to be "righteous." *This refers to living a life according to God's will.*

2 Corinthians 9:11—You will be rich in every way so you can be generous. *Ask students to share a time when giving filled them with joy.*

2 Corinthians 9:15—The ability to give what I have given you is also My gift to you.

CLOSING (5 MINUTES)

Invite students to write on scrap paper or on the back side of their Student Page one way in which God has shown His generosity to them. Use these in a closing litany of praise. As the leader reads each item saying, "For . . . ," the group responds, "We thank You, Jesus."

Encourage individuals to spend time evaluating God's generosity to them and their response. Remind them that we give God our time, talents, or money in response to His love for us. Discuss ways in which your students can respond to God's love in service to others.

9. Feed the Poor? I've Got Expenses!

True or Change It

Use the Bible passages to help you decide if the following statements are true. If they aren't, change the underlined words to make them true.

1. Everything I have belongs to <u>me.</u> Psalm 24:1

2. Sharing what I have with others is <u>my obligation as a Christian.</u> 2 Corinthians 8:3–4

3. God became poor so <u>He would know what it's like.</u> 2 Corinthians 8:9

4. Those who have more <u>should give more.</u> 2 Corinthians 8:12

5. We give to others who are in need so <u>God will love us more.</u> 2 Corinthians 9:12

Great Givers

Name the Bible characters who might have made the following statements. Use the Bible references if you need help.

_____1. *"I ordered the people to stop giving because they gave so generously we had more than we could use." Exodus 36:6–7*

_____ 2. *"The offering I gave was very little, but Jesus said it was more than anyone else gave." Mark 12:41–43*

_____ 3. *"Jesus was pleased when I gave Him my expensive perfume." John 12:3–8*

_____ 4. *"Even though we were very poor, we begged Paul to let us give money to the Christians in Jerusalem." 2 Corinthians 8:1–5*

_____ 5. *"Because of My great love, I gave the best I had to people who didn't even know me." Romans 5:8*

a LOVe LetteR

Use the Bible verses to finish the letter.

Dear _____ (Write in your name.)

    I love you so much that I died for you! I have all kinds of exciting things planned for you—far better than you can ever imagine! Someday we will be together forever in heaven.

    I want you to love Me too. Put Me first in your life. Don't let the things I've given to you become more important to you than I am. One way that you can show your love for Me is to share with others the things I've given you. With My Spirit at work in you, this can be one of the most joyful things you do!

    I know that even though you will try to put me first and share with others, you will fail because of the sin you were born with. Know that because of my Son, Jesus Christ, and His death and resurrection for you, I will always find you acceptable and pleasing in my sight. When you sin, I will forgive you. When you are overcome by temptations, I will help you and give you strength. When you give to others, you will do so because my Spirit will make you able. Trust in Me—rely on Me!

I give you these promises:

2 Corinthians 9:6 _____

2 Corinthians 9:8 _____

2 Corinthians 9:10 _____

2 Corinthians 9:11 _____

2 Corinthians 9:15 _____

Love from your Savior,

Jesus

10

FINDING THE TRUTH
IN GOD'S WORD

LESSON FOCUS

As young people grow in their knowledge of and interest in Scripture by the Holy Spirit's power, they will benefit from knowing the basics of biblical interpretation—Scripture interprets Scriptures, clear passages interpret unclear ones, passages have one central meaning, Scripture does not contradict itself, and others. By the grace of God these tools can enrich those who study the Bible as they grow as the Holy Spirit works through the Word to strengthen their faith.

GOSPEL FOCUS

The Bible, the Word of God, has an unchanging message of grace for all people—salvation through Christ and abundant life. Its message does not change, but it has new meaning and relevance in every age for those who read it with eyes of faith, enlightened by the Holy Spirit.

Lesson Outline

ACTIVITY	SUGGESTED TIME	MATERIALS NEEDED
Opening	5 minutes	Bible, hymnals
Clear Vision	10 minutes	Sunglasses, eye chart, petroleum jelly, Bibles, newsprint, and markers
Basic Principles of Interpreting Scripture	10 minutes	Copies of Student Page
Putting the Principles into Practice	15 minutes	Copies of Student Page, Bibles
Application to Personal Bible Study	10 minutes	None
Closing	5 minutes	Bible
BONUS SESSION		
The Good Book for Terrible Times	10 minutes	Copies of Bonus Student Page, newsprint, markers, Bible
A Good Book for You!	10 minutes	Copies of Bonus Student Page, Bibles

A NOTE TO THE LEADER

When helping young people find tools to better understand Scripture, it is important to give them guidance. Most teens are not ready to discern the difference between general Christian commentaries, Bible dictionaries, and so forth. Help students find resources that approach the study of Scripture from a Lutheran understanding. Visit www.cph.org for more information and available resources.

OPENING (5 MINUTES)

Read Psalm 119:105 and discuss ways that God's Word can provide "light" to our lives. Pray for God's Spirit of understanding. Sing "Thy Word Is a Lamp" (*All God's People Sing! [AGPS]* 247) or "Thy Strong Word" (*Lutheran Worship* 328; *AGPS* 246).

CLEAR VISION (10 MINUTES)

Say: "People wonder how we can be sure that we interpret the Scriptures correctly, when others use the same Bible to teach very different things. I need a volunteer to help me illustrate the problem." Choose a volunteer. Have him or her stand at one end of the room. Give the volunteer sunglasses with petroleum jelly smeared on the lenses. Go to the opposite end of the room (at least 10 feet away). Display an eye chart. (You can create one using black letters of various sizes from two inches down to one-quarter inch in height.) Compare how well the volunteer can read the chart with and without the sunglasses on. Allow others to try it if you have time.

Then say, "Our sinful nature is like the petroleum jelly, which distorts our vision. Because of sin, we cannot perfectly understand God's Word. God's Word is clear and true, but we need assistance in understanding it fully. Let's read what God's Word says about itself."

Form groups of three to five students. Give each group a sheet of newsprint, a marker, and a Bible. Assign each group one of these texts: John 17:17; 2 Timothy 3:15–17; and John 7:43, 47. Direct them to write several truths that these verses teach about God's Word.

When they are finished, have each group display their findings. Add the following key concepts if they are not clear.

John 17:17—Christ assures us that the Word of God is truth. Ask students to name someone who is trustworthy enough that they can say, "What he/she says is truth."

2 Timothy 3:15–17—God's Word is God-breathed. Scripture is inspired by God—given directly and precisely by Him—so we can expect it to be clear rather than mysterious or inaccessible.

John 7:43, 47—Only those who believe God's Word can truly understand God's Word. Without faith in Christ, it is impossible to interpret Scripture correctly.

Then say, "We can trust the Bible. A few basic principles will help us to hear what Scripture says, while avoiding human interpretations or prejudices."

BASIC PRINCIPLES OF INTERPRETING SCRIPTURE (10 MINUTES)

Distribute copies of the Student Page and read the introductory paragraphs, which highlight the several basic principles.

Then say, "This is not a complete list, and it may not answer all the questions about our use of the Scriptures. But as our starting point, these principles can help us read God's Word and understand the message God intends. Some other religious groups rely on other 'keys' for 'unlocking' Scripture. These may include 'personal revelation' or feelings, the teachings of a charismatic leader or council, or reliance on human reason and understanding. These other 'keys' can be helpful only if, and only to the extent that, they are in agreement with the Bible and what the Bible teaches about itself." Point out that using other resources as an aid in understanding the Bible is not wrong and, in fact, can be helpful, provided that (1) those resources are prepared using sound principles of interpretation and (2) the Bible is always the final authority.

PUTTING THE PRINCIPLES INTO PRACTICE (15 MINUTES)

As a specific example of using these principles, direct the students to read the Bible passages and discuss the questions on the Student Page.

Revelation 20:4–8 is the basis for great confusion among Christians regarding Christ's second coming. By itself, it seems to say that Jesus will return to the earth some day to rule for a 1,000-year period, after which Satan will continue his destructive work until yet another return and the final judgment by Christ.

In John 6:40–44, Christ teaches a "single step" return and resurrection. Say, "These two texts seem to contradict each other. Any ideas of how to pull them together?" In the discussion, apply the principles of interpretation. Point out that we begin from the clear words of Jesus in John 6 (and other places, such as 1 Thessalonians 4:15–17) to understand what the Bible teaches about the time frame of His return. Because the entire Book of Revelation relies on symbolic picture language, we understand the 1,000-year reign of Christ in Revelation 20 to be symbolic rather than literal. Based on the rest of the Bible, we find that the main point of Revelation 20 is that Jesus has not left His people unprotected. Satan is powerful, and it often seems that he has gained control of our world, but we can be sure that Jesus continues to restrain Satan's ability to harm His church and His people.

APPLICATION TO PERSONAL BIBLE STUDY (10 MINUTES)

In small groups have students brainstorm answers to these questions: Why might it be difficult for you to apply these principles by yourself? What types of activities or resources could help you use them in your own personal Bible study? After a few minutes, invite reports from the small groups. Answers to the first question include our sinful condition, which makes us spiritually blind and easily distracted, and our limited knowledge. In discussing the second question, note the value of using materials (devotions, Bible studies, commentaries, etc.) that respect and utilize the principles of interpretation. Note also the importance of continuing to grow in understanding the whole Bible so students can actually put the "Scripture interprets itself" principle into practice themselves.

CLOSING (5 MINUTES)

Read 2 Timothy 3:15 again. Ask, "According to this passage, what is the main purpose of the Scriptures?" (They are given to make us "wise for salvation through faith in Christ Jesus.") Close with prayer. Thank God for the gift of salvation in Christ and for the gift of His Word, which reveals salvation to His people.

bonus session

THE GOOD BOOK FOR TERRIBLE TIMES (10 MINUTES)

Distribute copies of Bonus Student Page 10. Ask a volunteer to read 2 Timothy 3:1–5. Tell the class that Paul mentions at least 20 different sinful behaviors and attitudes that people are likely to get caught up in. Challenge the class to identify these vices. Appoint two recorders to maintain the list on newsprint or the board. (Recorders should alternate writing responses so that the list may be compiled quickly.) Encourage your class to share these behaviors and attitudes in their own words. For example, "lovers of themselves" might be listed as self-centered or egotistical; "lovers of money" as greedy; "boastful" as taking credit for God's blessings and gifts; "unholy" as showing no special respect for God; "not lovers of the good" as troublemaking;

"lovers of pleasure" as worldly and unspiritual. Make certain that students realize that "having a form of godliness but denying its power" means being Christian in name only—participating in "religious" activities but having no personal faith in or relationship with the Lord.

Once the entire list is compiled, thank the recorders and have them sit down. Go through the list, one by one, and ask students if that attitude or behavior is still around. Direct students' attention to how Paul warns Timothy to respond to people caught up in these behaviors. Ask students how following Paul's warning would affect their lives. (Are there friends or family members with whom they would not be able to hang around any more? Which of their own behaviors and attitudes would they have to repent of and ask God to change?) Allow volunteers to respond briefly.

Direct the class to read 2 Timothy 3:14–17 silently and consider how God's Word can help us with evil attitudes and behavior. After allowing adequate time, ask a student to read the passage aloud and allow students to share their answers. Encourage them to recognize that reading and studying the Bible not only teaches us right from wrong, but also reveals to us all that God wants us to know about His love and salvation for us through His Son, Jesus, and equips us to trust Him—even in terrible times.

A GOOD BOOK FOR YOU! (10 MINUTES)

Divide the class into pairs. If the class has an odd number of students, participate in the exercise yourself. Have your partner ask you the questions and answer them for the entire class to model the procedure. If you are not part of a pair, share your answers as an example before the interviews start. A sample answer: "A child in my neighborhood invited me to her church when I was eight. I began getting acquainted with the Bible then. So far, the Bible has equipped me to want to be honest, to watch how I speak and act toward others, and to pray instead of panic when I am afraid."

Then instruct the pairs to interview one another using questions 1 and 2 in this section. After the interviews, students should reassemble and report briefly on their partners. After the reporting, have students return to their partners and work together on an answer to question 3. When the pairs have finished, reassemble the class and ask a spokesperson from each pair to share their answer.

After all pairs have reported, direct the class to turn to John 20:31 and read the passage aloud. Ask students to explain what being "the Christ" and "[having] life in His name" means. Students should be able to state clearly that Jesus died for us, accepting the penalty for all humankind's sins, and all who know Jesus saved them from eternal punishment and trust in Him have new and eternal life.

10. Finding the Truth in God's Word

Basic Principles of Interpreting Scripture

Since Scripture is given by God Himself, we can be sure of these things:

1. God's Word is clear. (God wants His people to understand it.)

2. A passage of Scripture will have one central meaning. (We don't look for new and creative things that a passage might say. The meaning God intends will not change with time or circumstance.)

3. The Bible interprets itself. (We trust the parts that are easy to understand to explain the more difficult parts.)

4. The Bible is understood by faith. (When its teachings seem impossible, we trust the words rather than our mental abilities.)

Putting the Principles into Practice

*Read **Revelation 20:4–8.***

If this were the only thing we knew about Christ's second coming, what conclusions might we reach?

What does it seem to say about the time frame of the resurrection?

What parts of this passage make it confusing or difficult to interpret?

*Read **John 6:40–44.***

What does this passage say about the time frame of the resurrection and Christ's return?

How does the time frame in this passage differ from Revelation 20?

Using the principles above, how should we deal with these two passages?

Which of the two passages seems clearer?

*If we recognize **Revelation 20** as "picture language" rather than take it literally, what might it mean?*

the good book for terrible times

*Read **2 Timothy 3:1–5, 14–17**.*

1. What is Paul warning his young friend and fellow believer, Timothy, about?

2. Is Paul's warning still appropriate for your life today?

a good book for you!

1. Timothy was taught the Scriptures from the time he was a young child. When did you begin to get acquainted with the Bible?

2. List some specific ways in which God's Word has equipped you so far:

3. There is one basic "exam question" for all Bible students: Why did God have the Bible written in the first place? What's your answer?

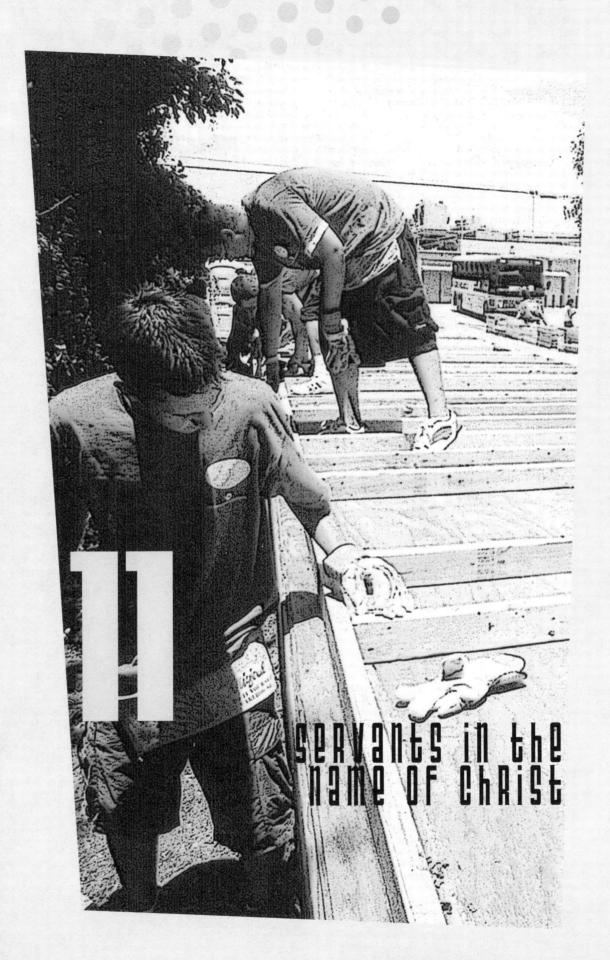

11

servants in the name of christ

LESSON FOCUS

In a powerful prelude to the Last Supper, Jesus demonstrated the nature of Christian service as He washed the feet of His disciples. Hours later in the greatest act of service, Jesus defeated sin and made it possible for His people, empowered by the Holy Spirit, to "wash the feet" of others. Christian young people will respond to challenging opportunities for service as they grow in faith through Word and Sacrament.

GOSPEL FOCUS

As God changes the lives of young Christians through His Word, He also will empower them to be servants in Christ's name to those who need to experience God's love and care.

Lesson Outline

ACTIVITY	SUGGESTED TIME	MATERIALS NEEDED
Servant Roles	10 minutes	Help-wanted ads from a newspaper, newsprint and markers
Greatness through Service	10 minutes	Copies of Student Page, Bibles
Jesus' Serving Example	15 minutes	Copies of Student Page, newsprint
We Serve	15 minutes	Newsprint or whiteboard, servant events information (optional)
Closing	5 minutes	None
BONUS SESSION		
Servant Jesus	10 minutes	Copies of Bonus Student Page, Bibles
Servant Me	15 minutes	Copies of Bonus Student Page, Bibles
Servants Together in Christ's Name	15 minutes	Copies of Bonus Student Page, Bibles

SERVANT ROLES (10 MINUTES)

Greet each participant as he or she arrives. Direct the students to the classified ads. Have them begin to clip ads that interest them. Talk about their futures, about jobs they may be considering as vocations, or about jobs that they currently hold.

With the students' help, make a list of jobs on newsprint or on the board. Talk about what they offer. Include such jobs as nurses, teachers, ministers, cleaning people, food preparation, child caregivers, bankers, scientists, architects, and others. Then ask, "What qualities are important for those who serve others?" List them on the newsprint or on the board as well. Help students recognize that compassion, caring, listening, dedication, understanding, responsibility, integrity, humility, and empathy are important qualities for those who serve. Remind students that whatever occupation someone has, they are able to serve others and God by being faithful workers.

GREATNESS THROUGH SERVICE (10 MINUTES)

Distribute copies of the Student Page. Direct students into groups of three to five to respond to the questions in this section. After a few minutes, invite volunteers to respond.

1. and 2. Name occupations that are highly valued or considered prestigious in our world today. Are occupations that involve serving others among the most highly paid or the most prestigious? Why or why not? (Students will see that, for the most part, service-oriented jobs are not necessarily the highest paid or the most revered today.)

3. Often the world's ideas of greatness and God's ideas of greatness are very different. Read Mark 10:35–45, especially 43–45. Summarize God's definition of greatness. (The Bible suggests that greatness is characterized by service. Expand discussion by saying, "Jesus demonstrated that servant role by suffering on the cross and dying in payment for sin—your sin and mine. By His service we are forgiven and empowered to put others first in our lives. His Spirit is at work in us as we hear the Gospel and as we are motivated to respond to it.")

4. What does this mean for you? How does it impact your life? Give examples. (Encourage students to think of situations when it is hard to put others first or to maintain a servant attitude. [For example, when we are in the cafeteria line, cleaning up after the ball game, or changing a baby's diaper].)

If you have time, invite the students to create situations and role-play them.

JESUS' SERVING EXAMPLE (15 MINUTES)

Assign this activity to be done individually. Or give small groups newsprint or poster board and markers and let them create a larger piece to display and describe. The verses listed examine Jesus' life for examples of service, including various miracles, His service of foot washing, and the events of Holy Week as He gave Himself up to death on the cross. Students are to create a collage of key words or symbols of these servant events. After 10–12 minutes, invite individuals or direct the small groups to share their work.

WE SERVE (15 MINUTES)

Say, "Jesus gave us a wonderful example of service, but we cannot follow it on our own. The Holy Spirit's power in our lives makes it possible for us to undertake forms of service."

On newsprint or on the board, brainstorm with the group examples of servant activities. Many churches receive information about national or regional service opportunities. You could share this information if it is available. Students can look at their own church, church family, and community for servant events. For example, youth could paint (Mrs. Jones's) trim since she is a shut-in, students could baby-sit for Pastor's church information class, students could rake leaves for (Mr. Brown), or the class could adopt a section of highway to keep clean.

Encourage the students to choose and plan one of the activities as a way to live out their servanthood. Help them set a date and meet as a class to embark on servant activities. All that we do as God's children is God-pleasing because of Christ's ultimate service. Begin your project with a prayer for the Holy Spirit to give you the attitude of service.

CLOSING (5 MINUTES)

Read Luke 9:48b: "[Jesus said], He who is least among you all—he is the greatest." Ask the students to pray silently for the Holy Spirit's power to carry on their chosen servant activity. Close by singing "Lord, Whose Love through Humble Service" (*Hymnal Supplement 98* 882).

bonus session

SERVANT JESUS (10 MINUTES)

Form small groups of three to five students. Distribute copies of the Bonus Student Page. Read, or have volunteers read, John 13:3–5. Then have the students share responses to the three questions in their groups. After a few minutes invite small groups to report on each question. As they do, share the following comments.

1. What service did Jesus perform? (Jesus did the work of a household servant, a very menial task.)

2. Why did He do this? (Point out that Matthew describes bickering among the disciples concerning importance and position just a week before this event in Scripture (Matthew 20:20–28) and that Judas will shortly leave to betray Jesus (John 13:18–30). Jesus very quietly sets an example of service for His disciples—and for us. His message for the disciples was to be servants themselves—to one another and to others. This message is also for those of us who by faith are disciples of Christ.)

3. Is anyone "too good" to be a servant? Why or why not? (Jesus is clear that as "the Master," He is not above service and that no one else is either. Point out that Jesus was our ultimate servant when He willingly went to the cross to suffer and die for our sins.)

SERVANT ME (15 MINUTES)

Follow the same procedure with this section: read Matthew 25:31–46, allow small-group discussion, and then invite reports to the group.

1. List six examples of servanthood Jesus mentions in this passage and give contemporary examples of each. (The six examples of service are feeding the hungry, giving drink to the thirsty, housing strangers, clothing the needy, caring for the sick, and visiting those in prison. As students suggest contemporary examples, press them to be realistic and concrete: taking food to a specific local homeless shelter, operating a free lemonade stand in a busy local park, befriending the newest student at school, bringing good clothes to class to deliver to a thrift store or needy family, distributing large-print devotional literature at a local senior care facility, or hosting a birthday or holiday party at a juvenile detention facility.)

2. Think of a time you helped others in a similar way, and share it. (Affirm any examples of personal service students offer, and seek as many details as you have time for.)

servants in the name of christ

3. List three characteristics of a servant. (As students share characteristics of servants, affirm positive ones such as selfless, loving, and outgoing, but also accept or suggest unexpected but realistic ones such as nervous or reluctant. Point out that being a servant can be an uncomfortable experience and still be very beneficial.)

SERVANTS TOGETHER IN CHRIST'S NAME (15 MINUTES)

Read Galatians 2:20 and seek responses to the questions on the Student Page from the whole group. Include the following comments.

1. When we believe in Christ as our Savior, what happens? (Christ lives in those who believe in Him. This is a miracle we can understand only through faith. Paul says that through the power of the Holy Spirit at work in us, we die with Christ—that is, our old nature is drowned in Baptism. Through His suffering and death—His ultimate service—we have new life through faith. Because He lives in us, we are partners with Him in our serving. We willingly serve Him and others because He served us by His dying on the cross.)

2. What does this mean to us as servants of Christ? (When we have faith in Christ, He lives in us. We live by <u>faith</u> in the <u>Son</u> of <u>God.</u> As servants of Christ we work motivated by His grace to help others.)

3. What power do we have to be true servants of Christ? (Christ's love for us gives us the power to love others. His sacrifice on our behalf changes us. It is more than our motivation to serve, it is also the source of spiritual strength we need for such service.)

II. Servants in the Name of Christ

Greatness through Service

1. Name occupations that are highly valued or considered prestigious in our world today.

2. Are occupations that involve serving others among the most highly paid or the most prestigious? Why or why not?

3. Often the world's ideas of greatness and God's ideas of greatness are very different. Read **Mark 10:35–45**, especially **43–45.** Summarize God's definition of greatness.

4. What does this mean for you? How does it impact your life? Give examples.

Jesus' Serving Example

In the space below create a collage of key words or symbols that will remind you of times that Jesus showed His willingness to serve. You can find helpful information in **Mark 10:13–16; Isaiah 52:13–53:12; John 1:14; John 2:1–11; John 4:1–26, 43–54**; other miracle accounts; and **John 13:1–17.**

Jesus was willing to put others first. With the Holy Spirit's power in our lives we can willingly serve others in His name.

Bonus Student Page II

Servant Jesus

*1. Read **John 13:3–5.** What service did Jesus perform?*

2. Why did He do this?

3. Is anyone "too good" to be a servant? Why or why not?

Servant Me

*1. Read **Matthew 25:31–46.** List six examples of servanthood Jesus mentions in this passage and give contemporary examples of each.*

2. Think of a time you helped others in a similar way, and share it.

3. List three characteristics of a servant.

Servants Together in Christ's Name

*1. Read **Galatians 2:20.** When we believe in Christ as our Savior, what happens?*

2. We live by _____ in the _____ of _____. What does this mean to us as servants of Christ?

3. What power do we have to be true servants of Christ?

12

the ChRiStiaN LiFe
can be a blaSt!

LESSON FOCUS

Some look at the Christian community and see a joyless people. Young people who see their Christian faith as joyless are misled. Sin works to destroy the joy that Christ intends for us as we work, study, and live in Him. Jesus died for the sin that would rob us of our joy and empowers us through His love to live joy-filled, abundant lives now and into eternity.

GOSPEL FOCUS

Through the study of His Word God's Spirit leads young people to confess the sin that would rob them of their joy and receive the joy that comes through Jesus' forgiveness. As forgiven children of God we can celebrate our Christian life and faith with abundant joy.

Lesson Outline

ACTIVITY	SUGGESTED TIME	MATERIALS NEEDED
Having a Good Time?	*15 minutes*	*Newsprint, blank paper, Copies of Student Page*
God's Gifts Are Great!	*5 minutes*	*Bible*
What Brings Joy?	*5 minutes*	*List from opening activity*
Joy in Christ	*15 minutes*	*Copies of Student Page, Bibles*
Closing	*10 minutes*	*Blank paper, newsprint*

HAVING A GOOD TIME? (15 MINUTES)

Ask students what they have been especially thankful for this week. Ask each person to write a list of 20 things that God has given him or her as gifts. Have each person rank the five best gifts on his or her list.

Create groups of three to five students. Have students share their individual list with the group. Create a group list of the top five items on newsprint. Post the lists from each group. Review them briefly with the class.

Ask, "Why are these things important to you? Would other people see these things as gifts from God?"

Distribute copies of the Student Page. Direct students to the list under this section. Have them rank the items in the list according to the instructions. The entire list will be ranked on the left. Only a few items will be on the right. Each list will be ranked according to the individual's preference. There are no right or wrong answers.

When most have completed their work, ask, "What do your rankings tell you about how you have fun?" (I enjoy my family, I enjoy being with friends.) "What could cause trouble in some of these potentially fun activities?" (We misuse them. Sin.) "Were any of your 'fun' activities potentially risky?" Let this last question be rhetorical unless you have some eager volunteers.

GOD'S GIFTS ARE GREAT! (5 MINUTES)

Read, or have a volunteer read, Genesis 1:31. ("God saw all that He had made, and it was very good.") Ask, "Is everything in the world still very good? If not, why not?" Students will likely point to the fall of Adam and Eve and the beginning of sin in the world. Then say, "It's not hard to see that sin is still very present in the world. Many of the things that the world considers 'fun' are in fact sinful. Some people measure their fun according to how risky or sinful an activity may be. From their perspective, religion is the opposite of fun. Let's take another look at fun."

WHAT BRINGS JOY? (5 MINUTES)

Direct the students' attention to the newsprint lists posted around the room. Ask, "Which of the gifts that we first placed on the newsprint are temporary sources of joy? Which of them can be taken away from us?" Use a marker to cross out the temporary items identified by the class. As the list gets shorter, you can help eliminate items with comments such as, "Friends often lose track of one another over time. When we grow old, even our good memories will fail." Then say, "Only those joys connected to our life in Christ are eternal. What are some of those?" (Students may suggest eternal life, Christian friends we'll see in heaven, etc.) Write these on the newsprint.

Some may suggest that the good works we do as Christians have eternal importance. The Bible tells us that God knows and rewards our service in Christ's name. The good works we do are the work of Christ in us. Stress that they in no way earn us salvation. Instead, our good works are a response to the salvation God provides us through faith in Jesus. (See Matthew 25:31–46 and Galatians 2:20.)

JOY IN CHRIST (15 MINUTES)

Read John 10:10. Ask the small groups to help brainstorm aloud what they think Jesus means when He says "life." Invite responses from each group.

Read John 15:9–12. Have the small groups discuss the remaining questions. Invite responses from each group. Use the comments below in discussion.

1. In what way can Christ's love make our joy complete? (As we relate to one another as brothers and sisters of Christ, all the things we enjoy have an extra dimension as they build our fellowship and glorify God.)

2. What can we say to a world that seeks joy only in temporary things? (Invite explanations of the student responses. If things get stuck, share Matthew 6:20–21. These verses speak about eternal treasure.)

3. How would you respond to someone who looks at the church from the outside and fails to see joy? (A sample response might be to encourage that person to take a closer look. Only through the eyes of faith can we see the futility of sinful pleasures and recognize the abundant life Christ offers us.)

CLOSING (10 MINUTES)

On the back of the Student Page, have students write sentences of thanks for the many blessings God has given to them. Encourage them to sign their names to these prayers of thanks. Have them pass these prayers around the group. Each person can add things that he or she is especially thankful for. Students can take their prayers home—with the added blessings—and pray for each other.

IF YOU HAVE MORE TIME

Have students list ways that they, their church, their friends, or their families can use the gifts of God to have a Christian "blast."

12. the christian life can be a blast!

having a good time?

To the left of the list below, rank the situations in the order of how much you think you would enjoy them.

___ The school homecoming weekend activities ___

___ Visiting your grandparents ___

___ Going out on a date ___

___ Going out to eat with your family ___

___ Spending the night at a friend's house ___

___ Going on a vacation with your friend's family ___

___ Attending a concert with your friends ___

To the right of the list, check the situations that present the greatest risk for becoming a "bad" situation.

Are any of these situations really bad or evil? What could make the situations you marked bad?

joy in christ

1. In what way can Christ's love make our joy complete?

2. What can we say to a world that seeks joy only in temporary things?

3. How would you respond to someone who looks at the church from the outside and fails to see joy?